MARGARET, Duchess of Argyll

My Dinner Party Book

MARGARET, Duchess of Argyll

My Dinner Party Book

Salem House Publishers
Topsfield, Massachusetts

Designed by Sheila Tugwell
Illustration by Eira Reeves
All photographs from the author's personal collection

First published in the United States by Salem House Publishers, 1986,
462 Boston Street, Topsfield, MA 01983

Produced by David Booth (Publishing) Limited,
8 Cranedown, Lewes, East Sussex BN7 3NA England.
Printed in Hong Kong.

Library of Congress Catalog Card Number: 86-61022
ISBN: 0 88162 223 0

The publishers wish to acknowledge the contribution made in
the preparation of this book by Mandy Bruce.

Contents

Introduction   7

Learning the hard way   9

The rules of entertaining   13

On the night   29

Entertaining the famous   33

Entertaining for other occasions   39

Entertaining at Inveraray Castle   51

The practicalities of entertaining   55

Menus and Recipes   81

Diary section   129

Conversion tables   158

Index to Recipes   160

Introduction

ONE of the things Duchesses frequently do is entertain. Some find it a terrible trial and, to be honest, are not very good at it. I am fortunate in that I love entertaining and without sounding too conceited, some say I am quite good at it!

Well, I should be – by now. I have certainly had enough practice. Over the years I have given hundreds of dinner parties and, despite the butler getting drunk once or twice and having to be helped to bed by the guests, no party of mine has ever been a disaster.

Since I first started entertaining I have kept a guest book – a record of whom I entertained, when, what I gave them to eat and drink, plus the odd comment to jog my memory of the evening. Apart from the obvious advantages of such a book – you can ensure you do not invite the same mixture of people too frequently or give guests the same meal –it is also great fun to look back through the diary later remembering happy times of the past.

My Georgian house in Mayfair, with its pine panelled dining room and long Italian walnut table, is now sold. But my dinner party diaries, all bound in red calf, are neatly stacked in the study of my penthouse in Grosvenor House where I now live. So I will never forget the exciting dinner parties I gave in that house during my thirty-three years there – or the famous and fascinating people who attended them.

Many women, I know, are somehow afraid of giving parties. Others complain that their parties never seem to take off but inevitably flop like an overcooked soufflé! Yet every one of your dinner parties can be a success if you know how. So here's my knowhow, my rules and, I think, the secrets of my success. I do hope it makes your entertaining much more enjoyable, and that you will make this your dinner party diary.

Learning
the hard way

I STARTED entertaining and, of course, giving dinner parties when I was 20 and married to my first husband Charles Sweeny, the golfer. London society considered Charlie and I the ideal married couple and gossip columnists who had followed my every move as a debutante, wrote, "She is the beautiful proof that the Bright Young Thing of 1931 can blossom into the perfect wife of 1933."

We mixed with the glamorous – including Gertrude Lawrence, Douglas Fairbanks Junior and Randolph Churchill. Cole Porter even mentioned me in his song "You're the Top", the big hit of his musical Anything Goes ... "You're the nimble tread of the feet of Fred Astaire, You're Mussolini, You're Mrs Sweeny, You're Camembert ..."

Nevertheless I prefer to forget about the dinner parties we gave then in our homes, first in Cadogan Square and then in a lovely Nash house in Regent's Park. Frankly, when I was married to my first husband, we gave the world's most boring dinner parties. Here, I feel I must point out that these were Charlie's dinner parties, not mine!

We were always couples of exactly the same age group, couples traipsing into dinner just like the animals boarding Noah's Ark. For a start all of us had known each other for years, and to add to the dreariness we also met constantly during the week so we had little to say to each other at dinner. The men talked solely of business or golf and the women of the trials, tribulations or delights of being young and newly married. If I ever ventured to suggest that we invite a writer, an actor, a politician or a diplomat – anyone different – Charlie would say "Oh no. What on earth do you want them for? They won't fit in."

I was the hostess but I have to admit that these dinner parties taught me a lot – what not to do if you want to give a successful party. Certainly I have been ruthless with my invitation list ever since.

So I prefer to forget my first experiences of entertaining. It was when I divorced Charlie in 1945 and moved into my house, 48 Upper Grosvenor Street, bought for me by my parents, that I really came into my own, entertaining in my way.

Now I was completely on my own and rather naive to boot. But I was keen to learn how to entertain successfully. I started by giving dinner parties for six, including myself. I found that once I could invite the people I liked instead of all the bores I had suffered before, and once I could really organise the whole thing

The Tapestry Drawing Room.

myself, I thoroughly enjoyed entertaining. And, I discovered, I was good at it.

At the start I found it daunting giving dinner parties alone without a man for support. Gradually I got the feel of it and if I say it myself most were outstanding successes — I know they were because the guests always stayed late! You can tell it has been a bad dinner party when everyone gets up to go at the earliest possible opportunity!

As every hostess knows, giving a dinner party is a vicarious pleasure. It is the guests who should enjoy themselves, not you. In fact if you do it probably will be a failure.

It can be agonizing — those first few moments when everything is ready and you worry that no one is going to turn up . . . They always do.

Finally and inevitably you heave a big sigh of relief when it is all over and the guests have gone. Now you can enjoy yourself, going over the entire evening once again in your mind and feeling smug that the party was such a success!

I have entertained dukes and duchesses, ambassadors and politicians and millionaires, actors and writers, great wits — but never bores. But it really makes no difference who you have invited — the secrets of a successful dinner party remain the same.

It does not matter if you have not much money to spend. Some of the best parties I have ever been to were given years ago by the interior designer Nicholas Haslam. He did not have much money at the time and lived in a studio flat in Chelsea. We had scrambled eggs and bacon, then bread and cheese, lots of wine and the best "golden oldie" records on the record player, and fascinating guests. Everyone had a marvellous time. It did not matter that it was simple. What counted was that Nicholas knew the secret of a good party and, as a result, people would fight for an invitation.

The rules of entertaining

THE truth is that many women giving dinner parties worry most about the things that matter the least – the food, the decor, the flowers on the table and so on. The food is not too important – as long as it is simple and good. As for the decor, most people will not even notice it and the only person who will have sweated over it is you!

People make a party

The most important ingredient of a successful party is People.

People make a party and the skill is putting together the right mixture. People come first and foremost, and then drink – lots of it. If people get drunk that is their lookout, but you must provide it and it must keep flowing.

With people you must be ruthless. Rule One – no bores. The men must all be interesting and the women must be intelligent, witty and/or beautiful. She may be your best friend but if she's plain and dull too bad – she does not come to the party. Incidentally, I am not too enthusiastic about women's luncheon parties, but love a lunch with one close woman friend.

Never have a party made up solely of couples. Of course you inevitably invite one, two or three couples and here you can run into problems. You can get a fascinating man whose wife is a deadly bore or the other way around and there's nothing you can do about it.

I know of one couple – whom I will not name but they are important, pleasant and good looking. But, and it is a big but, as soon as they arrive at the party a gloomy cloud descends. Everyone notices it. I invited them often and then finally stopped.

With another couple I know, the wife is very attractive and amusing but the husband kills any party stone dead. He never speaks. So I simply do not have them. It is not worth it.

Try to mix professions. By that I mean you do not want to give a dinner party entirely for accountants or doctors or lawyers. The inevitable will happen – all you will end up talking about is accountancy, medicine or the law! Do not worry whether people from different professions will get on – they will. If they are intelligent. Brain meets brain.

The late, Lady Diana Cooper at a party at Upper Grosvenor Street.

Any excuse to give a party is a good one. But giving a dinner party for visiting foreigners is one of the best. They add new blood and it inevitably stimulates conversation.

I particularly remember one very successful dinner dance I gave for 100 people at 90 Park Lane, the Grosvenor House restaurant, shortly after I moved to Grosvenor House.

My excuse on this occasion was to welcome two Lebanese friends, Nadim Dimechkie, who had been Ambassador here for 13 years, and his wife Margaret, to Grosvenor House. They had been searching London for an apartment. I recommended this hotel and they took one of the most sumptuous apartments in the building.

The dinner went very well and Lord Forte, the hotel's owner, and his wife Irene, were among the guests.

For dessert the chef tried something different. He served vanilla ice cream on a bed of dry ice. The smoke was dramatic, the effect very pretty, and everyone was most impressed. Joe Loss provided wonderful music throughout and 100 more guests came in after dinner.

Inviting foreigners you've met on holiday is a very good idea. The English in fact are notoriously bad at returning the hospitality of foreigners. We are famous for it. I know one couple who stayed with some Americans for a month but as soon as the Americans came to London they were suddenly out of town. A quick way to lose friends.

So mix professions and mix nationalities at your dinner parties — and mix ages. Age does not matter at all. You do not want to invite teenyboppers, but people in their twenties will mix well with people in their sixties, or seventies, even eighties. Older people can be just as much fun as young. I know many of my young friends would have given anything to attend a dinner with my dear friend, the late Lady Diana Cooper, whom I loved. She's was such good company, and very very funny. I was always happy to invite her to any party of mine.

Have as many single people as possible but if you invite a person on their own never allow them to bring a friend. You do not want anybody's friend at your party. He or she may be a terrible bore. It is your party invite only the people you know and like.

If you have lots of unattached people then the singles are always meeting someone new. But of course, if a couple are living together but not married, you must invite them as a couple.

Number of Guests

I would advise anyone to keep the numbers down to begin with and to keep everything as simple as possible. I gradually increased the number of guests to eight and then to ten, then fourteen, then eighteen, and by the time my children were growing up I was giving dinner parties for forty or even more and organising dinner dances for hundreds.

I began to devise my own rules. For example, I certainly think there are rules for the number of guests you invite. Obviously two is a wonderful number – probably the best dinner parties of all are the ones just for you and someone special! I think four is a bad number because you always end up talking to the same person – whoever is sitting opposite you. Six is a bad number for the same reason. You want to talk to all the guests, not just two or three, and with six people there are only three "changes" you can make.

Eight is not good either, because if the hostess sits at the head of the table and you stick to the man/woman/man/woman rule, you end up with another woman sitting opposite. Twelve and sixteen are bad numbers for the same reason.

Ten is ideal. You have a man, whom you have made your host for the evening, at the head of the table and a woman at the other end, and four either side alternately. It works too if you have fourteen or eighteen. There are plenty of different people to talk to and plenty of room to chop and change.

When to hold your party

Then, what night should you give your dinner party? I have found that Fridays and Mondays are the worst. People may be going away for the weekend in which case they are either just leaving, or they have just got back. Or, if they are staying at home, they are either exhausted at the end of one week's work or exhausted at the thought of beginning another. Tuesdays, Wednesdays and Thursdays are the best, plus Saturdays if people are not away in the country.

Lauren Bacall was a guest at my party for Arnold Weissberger and Milton Goldman.

Drinks and Tobacco

I had no idea about ordering wine and cigars. That had always been Charlie's job. But, as I have always found, you will never know unless you ask. If you go to a reputable wine merchant you get good advice and you will find that they are happy to give it to you. They like showing off their knowledge and once you start asking you discover there's no great mystery about it all.

I was particularly ignorant about alcohol since I never touched a drop until I was 30. I am still amazed by the fact that, as a debutante, I could dance the night away until the dawn rose over London — and all on nothing stronger than water, and not even a cigarette.

People think that the Bright Young Things of the Thirties drank a lot. In fact most did not — the Twenties were far wilder! I lived in America when I was in my teens but my mother insisted on bringing me back to London to "come out" because she saw how wild New York society had become in the Prohibition era. At parties she saw debutantes drunk with bad liquor called moonshine. So home we came — although as it turned out she need not have worried about me!

Cocktails are very much back in fashion — in fact I am told that they are almost as popular now as when I was a debutante in the Thirties. Personally I prefer drinks that are straight, not mixed, but many dinner party guests will be impressed if you serve cocktails before dinner — but more impressed by champagne.

My life has certainly been full of trials — in all senses of the word — but I honestly say that nothing, or no one, actually "drove me to drink". In the end it was simply boredom. I just got fed up with continually saying "No, I do not drink". Finally I said, "Hell! Yes!"

Even now there are many drinks I will not touch. I have never drunk brandy, vodka, gin or sherry in my life and I do not particularly want to. And I have avoided cocktails or, in fact, any mixed drink. I like to know what I am drinking.

Even now I never drink before seven in the evening — drinking at lunchtime ruins my day. But naturally I offer drinks to my guests.

So being a novice at the drinks cabinet, the wine merchant's advice to me was invaluable. I also learned quickly that the most expensive wines are not necessarily the best or the most appreciated. As long as it is a reasonable vintage, pleasant — and drinkable! — people are quite happy.

Many people worry about the drinks they should serve at dinner parties, but there are rules. Give guests two glasses of champagne before you go into dinner, then serve sherry with the soup, white wine with the fish course, red wine with the meat course and a champagne with dessert. But I would ignore most of this. If you cannot afford to serve champagne before the meal then offer whisky, gin and tonic or sherry. And if you cannot afford spirits serve red or white wine throughout the evening. Often I missed out the sherry with the soup and simply served red and white wine according to people's preference, but I always provided both. I do not like red wine so as a guest I will always keep on with white wine. (The most important thing is that the drinks keep flowing.)

I do consider smokers – I am one! (You must supply cigarettes for your guests.) I think it is extremely rude to smoke during dinner (a very American custom). It is unpleasant for the non-smoking guests and unfair on the cook. But the minute dinner is over cigarettes should be offered.

I asked the advice of a reputable tobacconist about which cigars I should offer to the men after dinner. No one ever complained so I presume I did not make any terrible gaffes. These days, though, I would never offer cigars to guests after dinner – they are so ridiculously expensive. If they want to smoke cigars, then I am afraid they have to bring their own!

I cannot emphasise strongly enough that it is much better to keep things simple and provide what you can afford, than to try to be grand and give a pretentious dinner party which you cannot.

Staff

Without doubt I certainly would never have managed those early days without the help of Mrs Duckworth, my wonderful housekeeper. Before long she was generally acknowledged as one of the best cooks in London and I have included some of her dinner party menus and recipes later in this book.

I cannot cook. I was brought up in an era when young ladies were not taught to cook and it was never expected that they should ever have to. Even now I never go near a kitchen. I hate raw meat, raw fish and raw eggs!

So if I had to give a dinner myself, I would serve cold food. And, as a guest, I would far rather have a good cold meal than an inedible hot one.

Mrs Duckworth stayed with me from the time I moved into Upper Grosvenor Street until she retired just a few years ago. I soon learned that there is no point, advantage or pleasure in serving a dinner comprised of dozens of courses. I have strict rules – three courses for lunch and no more than four for dinner. People do not need any more and you are only making more work for yourself – or your cook if you're lucky enough to have one.

The Drawing Room at Inveraray.
One of the many rooms our guests could enjoy during their stay.

King Umberto of Italy arriving at one of my dinner parties.

I have always been lucky in having staff who have been busy clearing away the dining room and washing up while I have been entertaining the guests in the drawing room after dinner. If I was not so fortunate, I would still be able to cope. I may not be able to cook but I am quite good at washing up.

Menu Planning

I never give big portions – people do not like them and with four courses you do not need them. I hate it in America when they give you a great big T-bone steak which is larger than the plate. I do not want piles of anything so I never give piles of anything. I have always been able to eat what I like without gaining an ounce but by choice I eat little. Funnily enough I find that men eat a lot. I am always surprised. What do they want with all that food?

For dinner we would usually start with soup, then a simple fish course, a roast meat or game course with a good rich gravy – thin, weak gravy is so awful – and a dessert. Never cheese. I think cheese should only be served at lunch. Dessert is the least important course. Many people, particularly women, are not much bothered whether they have a dessert or not but most men love puddings! Mrs Duckworth's pineapple dessert was an absolute triumph! After dessert I serve a large dish of cherries or grapes, but that was as much for looks as anything else.

Having foreigners to dinner did not affect the menu I devised in the slightest. I never included foreign dishes. Quite frankly, I think people just have to take what you give them and like it and when people are in England they should eat English food. In fact I think English food in homes and restaurants is very good these days.

Etiquette

Etiquette is something we can all fall down on – myself included. One of the worst gaffes I ever made at a dinner party occurred when I invited two ambassadors and the Lord Chancellor to dinner. The Lord Chancellor at the time was Viscount Kilmuir – a comparatively lowly title – so I put the two ambassadors on either side of me, and I put Lord Kilmuir in the middle of the table (in fact, "below the salt"). I thought the dinner went very well and was rather congratulating myself on it until another guest wrote telling me I had made a terrible mistake. After royalty, and the Archbishop of Canterbury, the Lord Chancellor precedes everybody, even the Prime Minister. He should have been sitting on my right and not below the salt. I was devastated! So I wrote a grovelling letter of apology to David Kilmuir saying I was so sorry to place him wrongly. He wrote a gracious letter in return saying he could not have cared less and adding how much he and his wife had enjoyed themselves.

If I had seated him in the correct place on my right, I would have had to put the most senior ambassador on my left. This is always the ambassador who has been in this country the longest, whether it be Pago Pago or the U.S.

So I suppose the moral of the story is – never invite the Lord Chancellor and two ambassadors to your dinner party at the same time.

Invitations

I invite people by telephone, instead of using invitation cards. If the cards manage to survive the post, people are so slow in answering. So I telephone and send reminder cards a couple of days later – that way people have no excuse for forgetting! Reminder cards are simply invitation cards on which you cross out 'To invite' and substitute 'Pour Memoir' or 'To Remind'.

Writing invitations and addressing the envelopes is full of pitfalls so these undisputed rules may help –

Rule 1 Even if you are inviting a couple – you address the envelope to the wife only.

Rule 2 If a single man has decorations you put them on the envelope only. Also the prefixes – The Rt. Hon. or Hon.

Rule 3 If you are inviting any Peer or Peeress, you put Lord and Lady on the card and the full title, such as Marquis or Countess, on the envelope. The only exception to this is when inviting a Duke or Duchess (or both), they must be addressed as that on both card and envelope, and with the addition of H.G. on the envelope. There is no informal alternative, I'm afraid.

If the Peeress is widowed or divorced she puts her Christian name – ie Margaret, Duchess of Argyll to differentiate her from the present Peeress. The alternative

Myself and Patrick Lichfield.

prefix is Dowager, which is reserved for the mother of the reigning Duke.

Rule 4 Surgeons and specialists are addressed as Esq. (as apposed to Doctor).

Invitations should always have a first class stamp on them. The easiest way is to invite everyone by telephone if possible and if they accept, send the invitation card but strike out the R.S.V.P. and put "TO REMIND" instead. To be correct, the invitations should be engraved, not printed.

Incidentally, I have been amazed by the number of people who should know better who spell Argyll, as Argyle.

I never accept any invitation that is not addressed to me in my own name. I would not dare, it is courting disaster. This rule is engrained in my mind because of something that happened to me many years ago as a debutante in London.

One of my young admirers was Viscount Selby and he had an invitation to a ball given by Viscountess Cowdray. Tommy Selby invited me to go as his partner.

We had been dancing for no more than a few minutes when Viscountess Cowdray herself came up to me in front of everyone present and asked "Miss Whigham" (as I was then) "do you have an invitation to my dance?"

"No Lady Cowdray," I replied, "Lord Selby asked me to come as his partner." She turned to Tommy and said, "I do not remember inviting you to bring a partner, Lord Selby."

The humiliation! I fled from the ballroom, face bright pink and feeling absolutely crushed. My father called Lady Cowdray the next day – blew her up and insisted she apologised and she did, but I have never forgotten the incident.

Thank you's

The writing of thank you letters is a difficult matter. It is tedious and I really do not think people should have to write them too often. In Victorian times there was a custom that you only wrote a thank you letter if you had spent the night under someone's roof. Very sensible. These days people write them for cocktail parties – perhaps they have nothing better to do.

My rule is that you write a thank you letter only if you do not know your host and hostess very well.

Whether you're invited to a cocktail party, a dinner, a dance or a wedding, I think it is best to telephone your thanks instead of writing.

Many people send flowers as a thank you present after a dinner party, which is charming. But before the party would be even more appreciated so we can enjoy them on the night, rather than be swamped with flowers when there's no one to see them except the hostess.

Giving presents when you arrive is an American custom, and is very kind. I am told many people bring bottles of wine to dinner parties these days. If you are giving a very informal party that is obviously acceptable – but to bring bottles to a dinner party is almost rude. It is your dinner party – it is your responsibility to cater for your guests.

Be prepared

Preparation is another secret of the successful dinner party. The better prepared you are the more time you can devote to entertaining your guests and the better the party is likely to be. I think it is sad that at so many dinner parties these days the guests hardly see their hostess – she is always in the kitchen. Nor do guests want to see a flustered hostess, it makes them feel guilty and uncomfortable.

I always plan a dinner party several weeks in advance. At 48 Upper Grosvenor Street I gave Mrs Duckworth at least two weeks' notice – it was only fair to her. She had to do the shopping – order all the food, etc. I must admit I was never involved in that. I stay away from kitchens.

As well as preparing the food, the drinks and the table, the hostess must have time to prepare herself. I always give myself a good 45 minutes of "breathing space" before the guests arrive, to have a look around and check that I have not forgotton something. In fact anything can happen – guests might ring to say they may be late, in which case you have time to rearrange the table.

Before my breathing space I allow myself ample time to dress. Every hostess needs time to make herself look her best. If you feel you look your best you will feel more relaxed and the guests will sense this. Naturally dress is important – after all you hope to be the most attractive woman there!

At my dinner party for Arnold Weissberger, Joan Collins was one of the guests.

On the night

GRADUALLY as I became more experienced in entertaining, I found myself sticking to more rules. For example, I am very strict on time. I invite people for 8.o'clock then I allow 45 minutes for drinks before we sit down to dinner at 8.45. In those 45 minutes most people have time for two cocktails or glasses of whatever and that is enough. There's an awful habit in many countries of drinking solidly for hours before you sit down to the meal at ten or even later. Texas is one and Spain another and I think the custom is absolutely barbaric. For a start most people have drunk so much they are no longer interested in eating and in the second place it is not fair on the cook – who these days may well be you!

If guests arrive late, so be it – they only get one drink before dinner instead of two. If they are so late we have already gone into dinner that is just too bad – they do not get dinner! Most guests can be on time if they make the effort, or at least within 45 minutes and, if their car has broken down, or train has been delayed, they can always telephone.

The importance of punctuality was instilled into me when I was a very little girl. My parents were very strict with me. If I was just one minute late for lunch I was in trouble. It is a habit I find impossible to break and I am probably too punctual. It does have disadvantages. Many's the time I have driven around the squares of London making up the minutes before I can actually ring the doorbell. Even then nine times out of ten I am the first to arrive.

Once your guests arrive you have the problem of introducing everyone to each other. Guests have the infuriating habit of arriving in a bunch all at the same time and then lurking in the hall or doorway to the drawing room. You feel like saying "wait there, while I introduce so and so to so and so" but of course you cannot do that.

I always have music playing in the background at the beginning of the party – it puts people at their ease – I have the record player in the room next door to the room where the guests are gathered. If you have it in the same room the music instead of the conversation will dominate.

Once they have all arrived, and you've made the introductions and settled them with a drink, you still cannot relax. You have to keep an eye on everything all the time.

You must make sure the conversation keeps flowing, and see that nobody is left out. People say that you should never talk politics or religion at dinner parties and they advocate keeping away from tricky subjects. I think this is nonsense. People should talk about whatever they wish — as long as they do not insult each other!

You must especially make sure that no one is left with an empty glass — fatal. This can be difficult if you have a large party even if you have hired staff for the night or have a butler. Butlers are not always perfect.

You also have to make sure that someone is not being cornered by a bore and cannot get away. You have to extricate them because people are so stupid they do not know how to get up and fetch themselves a drink, and thus free themselves from the situation.

It is for you to lead the party into dinner — and it is your task to get up from the table first, thus indicating dinner is over. These are the ground rules.

During dinner there should be no pauses or gaps in the conversation if you have invited the right people. I had a few "regulars" whom I could call on to come to a dinner party and I know they would keep the conversation flowing smoothly. Never invite an extra woman. No woman wants to sit next to another woman at dinner. So for safety's sake it is a good idea to invite an extra man.

As a hostess you must try and draw people out and get everyone talking to everyone else. Obviously, guests have to co-operate. Americans are good and so are the French — they are great conversationalists. But many English men are particularly bad. If the person sitting next to them does not amuse them they will clamp up — I think that is very rude and uncivilised behaviour. I hope that I am a good guest. I can be seated next to anybody and I will always do my best.

Generally speaking, once at the table I will allow a flexible hour for dinner, rarely longer. Usually I will offer second helpings. Sometimes things get spilt on the table during dinner or something gets broken but it cannot be helped. Whatever happens, you, the hostess, must ignore it and just carry on smiling.

At the end of my dinner parties guests would often send their compliments to the cook through me, but of course they would never ask for a recipe — that is an insult to any cook and, anyway, Mrs Duckworth would never have enlightened them.

One of England's most infuriating customs is that of the men sitting around the table with their port after dinner while the women retire to the drawing room. I never used to allow the men to sit at the table for longer than fifteen minutes — just time enough for the women to go upstairs and freshen up before enjoying the rest of the evening. If necessary I would go down to the dining room and ask the men to come up and join the ladies.

Happily the custom is dying out. It is rude to the women — who do not go to a dinner party to end up sitting together gossiping like a gaggle of geese, and when I had staff it was very unfair on them because they had to wait for the men to leave the dining room before they could clear up.

I have been to country house parties where dinner has been over at ten and the men have sat there guzzling the port until midnight. It is a complete waste of an evening. There have been occasions when I have been so bored that I have just disappeared and gone up to bed!

Of course this habit also means that the women may miss out on the best of the conversation. I am quite sure that many deals have been struck over the liqueurs in my dining room after dinner – in fact I have been told this – but unfortunately the men always waited until we had left the room. Politicians particularly like to hold forth – and often come out with interesting statements – after a good dinner and plenty of wine. Without doubt the conversation always livens up after dinner. It is really the best time of the evening, especially in mixed company.

Once dinner is over I think most women want to go upstairs and comb their hair, reapply their make-up and freshen up. During that time the men can sit gossiping and drinking liqueurs and then the women come downstairs again and everyone should be together. One of my favourite ideas for this time of the dinner party is to invite a few people along for after dinner drinks. I would ask people who were going to the theatre or cinema to come in afterwards. This meant that you added new faces to your party and fresh conversation.

As I have said, the sign of a bad dinner party is when people cannot wait to leave, but of course you have to accept that if you're giving a dinner party mid-week, many people have to leave around midnight because they must go to work the following morning. In this case it would be very impolite to press them to stay. You can feel when a party has reached its conclusion. And fortunately guests can sense it too.

A great and dear friend of mine, Paul Getty. He was a frequent guest at my dinner parties.

Entertaining the famous

NEVER be afraid to invite two people whom you think might provoke one another – it always makes for an amusing and memorable dinner party. Noël Coward was a frequent dinner party guest of mine and, when I could, I invited Elsa Maxwell, the famous – often vitriolic – New York gossip columnist at the same time. Both considered themselves far cleverer than the other and it was great fun listening to them try and literally out-wit each other.

Both loved being the centre of attention, which is why it was lovely to see them together!

Noël was just as funny off stage and off paper as on. Of course his wit was very biting and he could be quite cruel at times, but I always felt that it was up to my guests to look after themselves – I never protected them in any way from Noël's sharp tongue.

Elsa took a dislike to Paul Getty for some reason and was always attacking him in her column. Out of devilment I once invited her and Paul to the same dinner party without telling Elsa that Paul was also coming. Elsa arrived first and her jaw fell when she saw Paul walk in. But after dinner I noticed that the two of them were deep in conversation – apparently friendly conversation what's more – and the next morning when she rang to thank me for the party she added mischievously: "Blessed are the peacemakers, Margaret. Paul Getty is charming."

She was right. Paul was a charming and fascinating man. But actually he was by no means the ideal dinner party guest because he was terribly shy. He was far better company if you dined with him à deux rather than in a crowd. He also had a very low voice and he was quite difficult to hear so I always put two people either side of him, whom I knew he liked and whom he could talk to quietly through dinner! But although he was shy he was certainly never a bore.

Paul loved being asked and he genuinely enjoyed my parties so I invited him whenever I could. People said Paul was mean because he kept a pay phone in the hall of his mansion. I must admit I thought he was a bad father and I told him so. Ironically, he was attending a dinner party of mine in 1973 when he heard by telephone that his eldest son George had died in Los Angeles. Paul was absolutely devastated – but very stoical. I think perhaps Paul may have been jealous of all his sons because they were younger than him. Strangely Paul died on the same day as George, one year later.

Cecil Beaton at one of my cocktail parties.

I think that tycoons like Paul are too preoccupied with business to spend much time with their children, although if I had to choose, I'd rather have a workaholic husband than an alcoholic one.

Since his death a lot of rubbish has been written about Paul. People asked: "Was he happy despite his millions?" What nonsense! His millions made him happy and he was never alone!

If you invite the very rich or the very successful, the very famous or the very powerful, to your dinner party they sometimes will want to hold the stage. Usually it does not matter because most people are interested to hear what they have to say.

Lord Mountbatten, as he was when I first knew him, was a good deal older than I but I saw quite a lot of him at one time. Naturally he was a fascinating guest and an attractive man. He was also conceited and his conversation was mainly about himself. But that was all right because people would hang on to every word he said. His wife Edwina was a beautiful woman, very glamorous and elegant.

Dickie Mountbatten lived such a dramatic life and was such a dramatic man. I heard of his death by car radio while touring across Utah and it was a great shock, but I think that somehow it was almost the right way for him to go — suddenly and dramatically. I am still very friendly with his daughter Pamela Hicks and her husband David, the interior designer. Unlike her father, Pamela is not a very social person. If you ask them both to dinner you usually get David and not Pamela, which is a loss as they are both charming.

I entertained many ambassadors and politicians in my house. People may think that they must be stuffy and boring but I have found none who are. How can anyone be boring who has been sent all over the world to represent their country? How can anyone be boring when they are so involved in the issues of the day and have so much inside information.

I have learned many fascinating things during entertaining when my political guests were relaxing among friends. Obviously they are not going to give away too many secrets — but they will exchange opinions about events of the day.

Anthony Eden was one frequent dinner guest and he would naturally dominate the conversation. If anyone was in power in the 1950s it was he. Yet strangely enough, although he spoke beautifully in the House of Commons he never actually impressed me with wit or pearls of wisdom in private. Compared to the figure he presented in public life he was almost dull.

His first wife Beatrice was charming but very unsocial — as you so often find in the case of women married to famous men. As a man he was more interesting than charming. But I liked him and of course such a prominent politician's presence always guaranteed a good dinner party. Anthony and I sometimes dined when he and his wife had separated.

I attended the opening party of interior designer David Hick's shop in New York.
Here we are with his wife Pamela, and his father-in-law, Lord Louis Mountbatten.

Duncan Sandys was a marvellous guest — always good company and always interesting to listen to, although he talked very slowly. He enjoyed being the centre of attraction and played up to it.

Greeks and Americans have always frequently featured on my guest list. I have met many Greeks through my friend 'Puggy' Vergottis and also through my many visits to Greece and I entertain many Americans, because America is my second home. I spent the early years of my life in New York, so I have a great affection for the country and the American people — my first husband Charles Sweeny was an American.

I knew many of the American ambassadors and politicians living in London. I met President Reagan briefly two years ago at the White House and he's just as he appears (on television), friendly and charming.

Jackie Kennedy's sister Lee Radziwill was a frequent dinner party guest of mine. A charming girl, good looking and marvellous company — in short a good guest! I always had the suspicion that she took a fancy to Aristotle Onassis before he actually married Jackie.

Strangely enough, later — but before he married Jackie Kennedy — Aristotle Onassis was one of my dinner party guests on many occasions.

He was a strange man, short and rather ugly. Other guests would kow tow to him. Women found him devastatingly attractive, partly I think because of his power and money. But if he had not had the money he would still have had great magnetism. (However the English may pretend, they are very impressed by money!)

Like Onassis, the Greek shipping magnate, Niarchos was not pretty but I found he had more charm than Onassis and he was one of my regular dinner party guests. But neither put themselves out to be charming — they felt they did not have to. Both men liked to be the centre of attraction but in fact they never held the other guests spellbound like Brendan Bracken, Hector McNeil — once Secretary of State for Scotland — or US Ambassador Lewis Douglas.

Entertaining for other occasions

THE word 'entertaining' is such a large one. It comprises dinner parties of course, luncheons – which I think are ridiculous events because everyone is always watching the clock and no one can relax; buffets – which I do not like so do not give – and brunches – which I also do not like, do not understand and therefore do not give.

I do not like so-called business lunches or dinners either. They seem a useless waste of time. If I want to talk business I will go to an office and talk across a desk.

Of course I appreciate that many women have to give dinner parties to further their husband's business careers. These parties are a gamble. The same rules apply for a normal dinner party, except that you cannot choose the guests so you cannot eliminate the bores.

Entertaining also includes cocktail parties which are now called drinks parties – an expression I dislike.

Then there are special–event parties. When Prince Charles married Lady Diana Spencer in July 1981, there were parties up and down the land – street parties, garden parties, dinners, lunches. I gave an after dinner party on the wedding eve, during the magnificent fireworks display in Hyde Park. My penthouse overlooks the park so my guests were able to get a wonderful view from my balcony, and we also had the fun of seeing the crowds in the park. I invited them to arrive after dinner and we drank champagne to celebrate the occasion.

I gave General Election Parties in May 1979 and June 1983. It was pointless having guests for dinner so I installed two extra TV sets in my apartment and invited any of my friends who were interested to come in after 10.30, changed or unchanged, and watch the results coming in, accompanied of course by flowing champagne. These parties sometimes lasted until early morning.

An important but different form of entertaining is the children's party. Now this usually involves a few children and their mothers – the children fighting each other to the death and the mothers ending up exhausted, but a good time is had by all.

In the past, some children's parties were quite grand and tea was served at the dining room table with each child having their nannie sitting beside them and controlling their grabbing sticky hands. Believe it or not, the children and their nannies were seated according to their rank! Formal as this sounds, the young had just as good a time and were just as destructive as now.

At a London dinner party with Bob Hope.

I have a hearty dislike for barbecues in full evening dress, which seem to be in vogue at the moment. I mean, if you're going to have a barbecue then it's fine if you're properly dressed for it and go out looking like someone from a cowboy film. But to go to a barbecue in a floor length dress in a field or London Square is totally ridiculous. Your shoes get absolutely filthy and so does the hem of your dress and it inevitably rains or has done the night before. So you wade around in the mud trying to look as if you're enjoying yourself, while all the time you're thinking about your dry cleaning bill or whether the damage to your dress and shoes will be permanent. It is difficult to look, feel or appear beautiful in evening dress at muddy barbecues.

Of course it is totally different if the barbecue is held in a beautiful country house with a paved terrace. But if you do not have a patio or terrace, forget it.

Dances used to be far more popular than they are now, probably because today they are so expensive to give. Yet most people at some time in their lives have to arrange a big party for some special occasion – a 21st, or a wedding or engagement party.

My daughter Frances's coming out ball at Claridges was a wonderful evening. By eighteen she was an enchanting beauty and for the evening she wore a lovely dress designed by Norman Hartnell. We had one hundred people for dinner and seven hundred for the dance afterwards. As you can see I had progressed quite a long way from merely having six people to dinner!

As it was given for a debutante we chose the colour pink as the theme for the decor. The overhead chandeliers were turned off (of course) and the wall lights were masked with pink. There were pink tablecloths, pink candles and pink flowers everywhere. It was a party that will always stay in my mind.

My favourite form of entertaining is to give a dinner-dance. An American innovation – it means that you have dinner at the same time as the band is playing and people dance between courses. Which I love.

The British tend to think that music puts them off the serious business of eating so they refuse to pay any attention to the music or dance until the liqueurs are served. So if you are giving a big dinner dance in England you have unfortunately to bow to this custom.

The secrets and rules of a successful dinner-dance are much the same as for a dinner party. Of course the preparation is that much more arduous and involved but there are several guidelines which I have devised and which, if you follow them, should help.

As with dinner parties, the secret of a good dinner-dance or wedding party is people – and plenty to drink. But to that list in this case you can add music. The music *must* be good and a live band is essential, if only a four piece one.

I know many people now have these discotheques at parties – but not me. Music has always been a very important part of my life. I think most music today is so

An evening to remember – Paul Getty's 80th birthday party at The Dorchester.
Amongst the guests were Tricia Cox (neé Nixon) and the Duke of Bedford.

awful – my era ended in the 1960s. I love the popular music of the late 1920s, 30s 40s and 50s. I am supposed to be quite an expert on the subject and have even been told that if fate had taken me along a different path I could have been a dancer.

I have a vast collection of 78s and some of them have been used to re-record the old songs for the present day, as in many cases the master recordings have been lost.

Even though Cole Porter wrote a verse about me in "You're the Top", I was never fond of his songs. Among my many favourites are "Say It Isn't So", "You Know That I Know", "Linger Awhile", and all the unparalled music from *Showboat.*

I have always thought that there are two things I would wish to save if the house caught fire – my dog and my record collection!

If you are hiring a band always 'audition' them before the big night if they have not played for you before. I remember for Paul Getty's eightieth birthday party I was hiring Joe Loss to play. I had employed many bands for previous parties but never Joe Loss.

The day before the party I insisted on rehearsing Joe and his band. He was absolutely furious. Obviously a bandleader of his calibre thought it totally unnecessary. But I said to him – "Mr Loss, we do not know each other and you do not know the kind of music I like, so let us get to know each other now rather than later at the party!"

The band turned up at ten o'clock in the morning at the Dorchester for rehearsal. They had been playing the night before, they were tired and fed up. "Right" I said, "play me what you would play for the party". So they did. And it was dreadful! Not that they were not all very good musicians – it was their tempo that was wrong; slow and dead beat, guaranteed to kill any party stone dead. I said "No, no, no! Faster, add a little pep and keep it like that. Keep the same tempo and do not stop for two hours and if any of you want to go to the loo you will have to go off one by one." Joe said "People will ask for pop music and waltzes." I said, "I do not care what people ask for, they are not going to get it." The party was a great success – due in large part to Joe Loss's music.

An example of the best kind of dinner-dance was recently given by Mr Rocco Forte to celebrate his 40th birthday in the ballroom of Grosvenor House.

All 350 of his guests were seated and placed at tables of 10 – no nonsense about a buffet snack that night!

Rocco had flown a band over from America, the famous Lester Lanin. They played fast and non-stop the entire evening and the guests danced all night. It made all the discos look silly.

I have learned from bitter experience that to keep a dance going you must have fast music all the time – without stopping. Of course after a couple of hours the band must have a rest, but then I used to try and arrange for some kind of cabaret to

I do love to give dinner dances. Here I am dancing with US Ambassador, Walter Annenberg.

I just decided to give a party, and one of the invited guests was Prince Michael of Kent.

come on. Afterwards the band would go back on stage and carry on playing fast tempo all the time. As soon as you change the tempo to a slower pace the floor clears quicker than you can say Joe Loss! It is disastrous.

Waltzes are the worst. The band is playing a good fast number and then suddenly they change to a waltz and the floor is deserted. People have been dancing and enjoying themselves and suddenly the change of tempo makes them think of returning to their seats, taking a rest and – worst of all – looking at their watches! They suddenly realise how late it is and think they'd better be going home. If the tempo remains the same they forget about time and do not worry. You really do not want people leaving a dinner-dance at midnight – far too early. It should go on until two o'clock and I think there's a very good case for banning wristwatches from all dinner-dances!

I also think that it is wrong to drop the tempo of the music and have a few romantic numbers at the end of the party. That's the time the tempo should be even faster if anything. When you stop the dance at two, three or four you stop it suddenly. The music stops, the lights go up and that is it. People feel tired but exhilarated. They mingle briefly saying goodbye and then they are gone. It really is much the best way.

Just as I sometimes rehearse the music at a dinner-dance I give, so I always test the food too if I am giving a party in a hotel. There is nothing worse than sitting there as hostess at a party for forty or four hundred people eating a meal which turns out to be wrong.

I always discuss my menu with the hotel or chef and then sample the actual meal that they will be serving on the night. Every time I have done this I have found something wrong with the meal. Either the cooking is bad, or more likely the meal is simply not as you have imagined it and therefore you are disappointed. There is always some little thing.

I have found that chefs have no objection to you asking to taste the meal before the actual party. They enjoy showing off their skills and they would far prefer for you to be happy on the night when you have a hundred guests. On "the night" it is all too late to correct mistakes.

I really do think the same applies when you take a large party out to a restaurant for dinner. Some people cannot entertain at home for one reason or another so taking people out to a restaurant is a perfectly acceptable alternative. If there are more than eight of you far better to plan the menu, test it and give them no choice just as you would at a dinner party in your own home.

I now live in a penthouse which is too small to entertain as much as I'd like to or, indeed, used to. So rather than have a few people at home I entertain them in restaurants.

Before the dinner I ring the restaurant and warn them about the dinner party and tell them the menu I want. Then several days before the actual party I go and have the meal for lunch – on my own! I suppose I must look quite funny to outsiders. I sit there and we're all very sombre – the waiters, the chef and I – but it is absolutely invaluable and essential when you're not sure what food you're going to be getting and therefore giving to your guests.

When I give a dinner party in a restaurant I stick to just three courses – fish followed by meat and then a dessert and coffee. With three courses you should always serve something more substantial than soup – ie, a fish course. We have a drink before dinner in the bar and go through to the restaurant for dinner and back into the bar lounge for coffee and liqueurs. Unfortunately that is not always possible in a restaurant – you may have to have drinks at the bar and coffee and liqueurs at the table.

For example, I recently gave a dinner party for ten at Maxim's in London. The evening began at 8 pm in the champagne bar where my guests were offered a choice of champagne, Buck's Fizz, Kir Royale or soft drinks, and canapés.

The menu I chose was terrine of smoked trout served with a horseradish cream sauce, roast rack of lamb and fresh vegetables, and to follow soufflé glacé au Grand Marnier, coffee and petits fours.

The liqueurs were green Crème de Menthe or Kümmel and the wines – white Sauvignon de Touraine and red Vacqueras.

Obviously you also arrange the financial side of things in advance too. The bill should then be sent to you or – drinks apart – paid in advance.

Several times I have entertained Lord and Lady Forte at "90 Park Lane", the famous restaurant at Grosvenor House where I live, which must keep the waiters on their toes as he owns the hotel! He's also my landlord. A charming man.

Another completely different form of entertaining is pubic entertaining. In 1974 I was approached by the British Tourist Board who told me that many foreign tourists, especially Americans, were keen to see private homes of historical interest in London. Their problem was that no private homes in London were open to the public. Could I help?

I was pleased to do so and on April 9th 1974 my house in Upper Grosvenor Street was "Launched" with a pre-launch cocktail party for friends and the press. I really had no idea how successful it would be but the party proved to be just the beginning – the whole project went very well. In two years, four thousand people visited my house – and loved every minute of it. The tours were carefully organised. The guests came in groups – sometimes as many as 60 at a time – on Tuesdays, Thursdays and Sundays at 6.00 p.m. and not in coaches, but in limousines.

I always made a point of being there and when they arrived I greeted them in the drawing room. It was all very informal. They were shown around the house –

Lord and Lady Forte at a Grosvenor House dinner dance.

which was historically very interesting, built in 1729 – and we talked often until 9.00 pm. I met some fascinating people; there were architects, interior designers and historians of all nationalities, predominantly Americans, Australians and Germans.

I enjoyed these evenings very much and did not find them hard work. All the guests behaved impeccably and came back a second time. I did not need to hire extra staff – I served only champagne or soft drinks and I already had a butler.

Entertaining at Inveraray

Entertaining in the Highlands is a very different matter to London parties or weekends in the Home Counties.

First of all I discovered during ten years as hostess at Inveraray Castle that you usually do not plan your guests – they plan to visit you. The west coast of Scotland is a long way from anywhere and our only neighbours were Lord and Lady Glenkinglas and Sir Fitzroy and Lady MacLean.

Friends usually telephoned to say that they were 'passing through' and could they stay with us. They might stay a night, a week or a month.

Meals had to be planned well in advance and salmon, fresh from the river Aora, one hundred yards outside the Castle, fresh strawberries and raspberries when in season, venison or grouse all from our own grounds were most popular.

Any guests of ours had to be taken to the eighteenth century beautiful Royal Borough of Inveraray and to Mr and Mrs Alec MacIntyre's famous tweed shop, and have a drink at the George Hotel or the Argyll Arms. They were then usually left to their own devices with a map and lots of instructions.

Ian and I had a lot to do all day but we looked forward to seeing our friends at meals and in the evenings – we also prayed that they had their own car!

Placement at the dinner table and equal numbers were unimportant but what was important was that it was a very comfortable, warm house to stay in, modernised by me.

Neither Ian or I play bridge or any game but conversation flowed and a popular feature in the library was an enormous, very difficult jigsaw puzzle left permanently on a card table which would fascinate guests for hours. I used to do my petit point which meant I could talk, listen and sew at the same time. Then there was the occasional picnic in breathtaking scenery and a visit to nearby Loch Awe.

I have always loved Gaelic music and early on I started arranging Ceilidhs in the Great Hall of the Castle, 88 ft high. Ceilidh is a Gaelic word described in dictionaries as "an informal evening of song and story telling". Anybody who has not lived in the Highlands will not know about a Ceilidh let alone how to spell it. They are gatherings of local people who sing traditional songs handed down from father to son – they are never written. There are no instruments and the voices form the orchestra. I would invite the Lochgilphead Choir over, who are one of the best in Scotland and winners of the Mod Gold Medal. I would also invite any of the

Ian and I in the grounds of Inveraray, with Skipper the spaniel and Laddie the labrador.

townspeople who wanted to come and join in the singing — they all did and they knew all the songs from childhood.

Two essentials were to light both log fires in the Hall and produce large amounts of whisky, and as this musical evening wore on the singing got better and better!

There was one memorable weekend when I received word from Paris that Arturo Lopez, the Chilean copper millionaire, his wife Patricia, Baron Alexis de Rede and Princess Ghislaine de Polignac were all coming on the Lopez's yacht up to Loch Fyne which is a sea loch and would be anchoring at Inveraray I was thrilled as they were all dear friends, but rather apprehensive at the idea of entertaining these most elegant and sophisticated Parisians in the Highlands. They proved to be the perfect guests because, being a highly intelligent group, they were fascinated by Inveraray which is filled with treasures.

When they dined I gave them (guess what?) salmon, grouse and fresh raspberries, all from our own grounds. I was afraid of their comparing this with those fabulous French dinners, but my French friends were all gracious enough to say that it was one of the best meals they could remember. They were also interested in hearing Ian talk about the Castle, the town and all its history. Ian was a good raconteur and knew about every stick and stone of Inveraray. I was quite knowledgeable about the present day but I never did get the Argyll ancestors straight.

The Ball we gave at Inveraray on July 1st 1958 was the first for 100 years and it was one of the most enchanting evenings I ever spent. We chose to give it in Royal Navy Week and there were many ships anchored up and down Loch Fyne.

Three were anchored very near the Castle and on the night of the Ball they were all lit up (I believe "dressed overall" is the nautical term). The Castle was floodlit, the night was very clear, it was a full moon and the result was fairyland.

Six hundred guests came from all over Scotland. The men dressed in their kilts and uniforms, this meant arranging where everybody stayed.

Donald Ross who owned "The Apperitif" in Edinburgh did a wonderful job of arranging the catering, although so far away. We had a pipe band for those who liked reels and a dance orchestra playing those Golden Oldies in another room. At five in the morning when the guests had gone, Ian and I drove up to the top of Duniquaich, the watch tower on top of the hill overlooking the Loch. In the old days it was used to guard the Campbells from their many enemies. We watched the sun coming up behind the Castle and the ships, still lit up, and we made a vow then that we would give a Ball every year. It was a magical night and one I shall never forget. However, sadly that was the one and only Ball and my last summer spent at Inveraray.

The practicalities of entertaining

Practically speaking, after your invitations, this is where the dinner party starts. Clever shopping makes for a good dinner. Food is not the most important ingredient for a successful dinner party but every hostess obviously wants the best food possible. It is a matter of pride.

Where my knowledge is lacking I have taken my own advice and asked the experts! So I would particularly like to thank my wonderful cook of the past 30 years, Mrs Duckworth, for all her contributions. Good cooks are traditionally loth to give away their secrets – I am grateful she has been good enough to share some of hers.

Shopping

At Upper Grosvenor Street we were lucky enough to have supplies delivered to the house. These days most women shop for the food themselves and the most important thing is to find a good butcher's shop, a good greengrocer and a good grocer where quality is high and you get personal service and advice.

Supermarkets are a convenient way to shop and with a fast turnover of food you can be sure that most produce is fresh. But you really cannot beat the shops where you become known and, as a regular and valued customer, you will always be assured of good service and supply.

Never be afraid to complain to the shopkeeper if you are sold something that is not quite up to scratch. It guarantees you will not produce something bad again. Remember you are the one who is paying, you are the customer and you deserve good service. On the rare occasions when our butcher sent us a piece of meat that was not of good quality, it went straight back.

Much of your shopping for a dinner party can be done days before the event. Only the fresh produce such as the vegetables, cream and fruit need actually be bought on the day. The meat can be the day before. The freezer is obviously a great help for any busy hostess and many dishes freeze well.

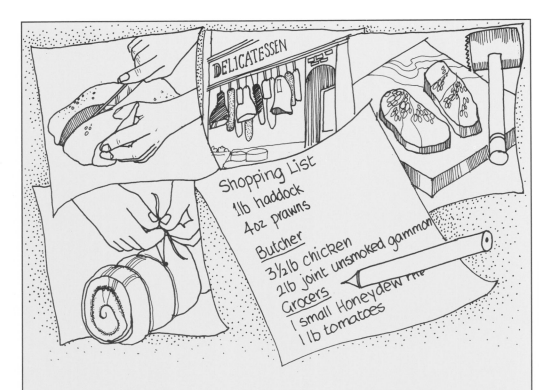

Within the image: DELICATESSEN

Shopping List
1lb haddock
4oz prawns
Butcher
3½lb chicken
2lb joint unsmoked gammon
Grocers
1 small Honeydew me
1lb tomatoes

Avoid economising by buying poor quality   It really is a false economy. Buy the best and you will find that apart from tasting good at the dinner party the meal stretches because you can use more of what you've bought, and the leftovers taste better too! So when you're shopping for your dinner party here's what to look for and what to avoid.

Meat: Find a butcher who sells prime meat ready for cooking. By that I mean that the meat should have been hung for the right amount of time. Even the very best quality meat lacks flavour and will be tough if it has not been hung properly. Ask your butcher's advice. A good butcher will be happy to give it to you — after all he is an expert.

Also, given a little notice, he will prepare special cuts of meat such as crown of lamb (complete with those pretty little white chef's hats on the end of each cutlet) or boned, rolled and stuffed pork.

As a general rule never choose meat which is too fatty.

Beef: The fat should be pale creamy yellow in colour and the lean meat should be bright red, slightly "marbled" with fat. This will keep the meat moist when it is cooking so it does not become tough. If you see gristle between the lean and the fat parts of the joint do not buy it. That usually means that the meat comes from an old animal. Roast beef and Yorkshire pudding really is one of the best meals in the world – although probably more suitable for lunch than dinner. That is up to you. But the best joints to buy in any case are rib or sirloin. We frequently had rib of beef. In either case allow eight to 12 ounces per person if the meat is on the bone or six to eight ounces if it is not.

Lamb: English lamb is delicious and available in early Spring and Summer. The fat should be a creamy colour and the flesh should look pink rather than red. Imported lamb can be bought all year round.

Veal: The flesh should be very pale, paler than lamb, and the meat should be soft and moist but not flabby and wet. There should be very little fat and what there is should be firm and creamy or pinkish white. Veal fillet is delicious and can be cut into thin escalopes (slices) which are beaten even thinner before cooking.

Pork: The fat should be firm and white and the lean meat pale and "marbled" with fat. Pork should always be cooked very thoroughly.

Poultry

Chicken: Many people use frozen chickens these days. How you cook the chicken and what it is going to taste like depends on how old it is. The older the bird, the tougher it will be. No chicken, old or young, should have a gamey smell about it. The flesh should be firm and the bird should also be nice and plump. You can tell if a bird is old or young by pressing on its breast bone. If the bird is young the bone will feel soft and pliable, if it is old the bone will feel hard and rigid.

Poussins are very small young chickens and you will need one per person. Broilers are also young birds, somewhat larger, which will feed about three to four people. Most frozen birds are broilers. Large roasting chickens are young cockerels or hens, weigh up to about five pounds and will feed five or six people. Boiling fowls are tougher, old birds and as this name suggests should not be roasted but boiled or casseroled. Capons are specially fattened young cockerels, can weigh ten pounds and the large ones will feed up to ten people.

Duck: In fact most of the ducks eaten are really ducklings, being under three months old. Older birds are likely to be tough. The bill and feet of the birds should be bright yellow – they darken with age. The flesh should be white and the breast nice and plump. Duckling is a very good dinner party dish, often tastier than chicken and delicious with sweet sauces like cherry or orange.

Turkey: Turkey can be eaten all year round, but of course it is the Christmas favourite. Again young birds are the best and the most tender so look for a bird which is firm and plump, has white flesh and smooth black legs.

Guinea fowl: Guinea fowls are in season all year but at their best between February and June. The fowl is actually a little bigger than a pheasant but smaller than a chicken. Look for the same signs of quality as for chicken. The guinea fowl needs to be hung before cooking. Use plenty of fat when roasting otherwise the flesh is too dry.

Goose: Goose is a big, delicious but very fatty bird. Another Christmas favourite. Once more go for a young bird with pinky flesh, yellow fat, soft yellow feet and bill. A ten-pound bird will feed about six people.

Game

Game makes delicious and impressive dinner party dishes. Roast pheasant has always been one of my favourites and Mrs Duckworth's recipe is included later. Game is the name for wild animals and birds which may only be hunted and killed when they are "in season". So here I have listed what you can buy when:

Grouse	August 12 ("The Glorious Twelfth") to December 10
Wild duck	August 12 to February 1
Partridge	September 1 to February 1
Quail and Pigeon	In season all year
Woodock	October 1 to December 20
Hare	August 1 to February 28
Venison	All year

All game birds should be hung before plucking and all should have a gamey smell about them. The more gamey the smell the stronger the taste. Fortunately most butchers now sell game birds which have been hung, plucked and are ready for cooking. Some game birds are sold frozen after their "in season" dates but undoubtedly fresh is best. Look for a young bird. If you choose a bird that is being hung in the butcher's shop look for soft feathers, plump breasts and easily pliable legs.

As a general rule all game birds should be cooked simply — roasted or casseroled. These birds should not be at all fatty so they need a lot of basting while being cooked. Many are sold already topped with some bacon fat which will keep them moist in cooking.

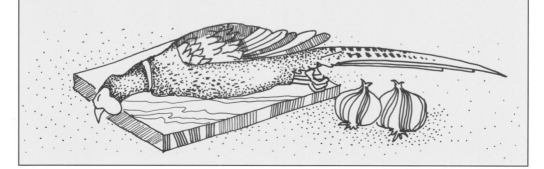

Fish

Fish is a traditional dinner party course. If you are giving people just three courses then the first should be more substantial than soup – fish or shellfish. And if you are giving your guests four courses then a fish course should follow the hors d'oeuvres or soup.

Fresh fish really must be fresh. If you are serving it at your dinner party you must buy it the same day. Good fish should be firm, covered with plenty of fresh-looking scales (if it is a scaly fish) and its eyes and general colouring should be bright. Fresh shellfish too must be eaten the same day as purchased.

Two of my favourite dinner party fish dishes are included towards the end of this book – sole with prawns and poached salmon. Like game, salmon has "a season". It is caught and sold fresh in England and Scotland between February and August. If you are buying a whole fish as a centre piece for a large party, look for one with a small head and broad "shoulders". The scales should be a silvery colour and very bright and the flesh should be a rich deep pink. When cooked the flesh goes a pale pink colour.

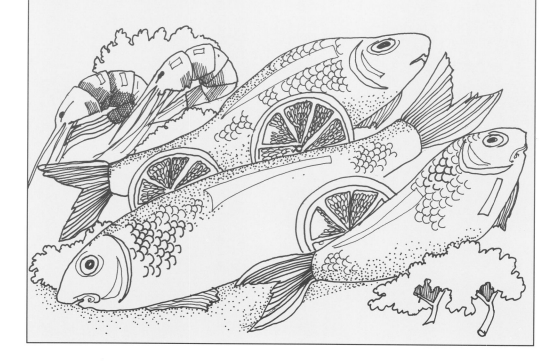

Vegetables

Frozen vegetables are a blessing if you are short of time but to my mind fresh are tastiest and they really do not take much longer to prepare. Choose your vegetables according to the season — runner beans in August/September, Brussels sprouts in the winter, etc. Buy your vegetables the day of your dinner party — the fresher the better. Keep them in a cool airy place and prepare them as near to the time that they are going to be eaten as possible. Serve them as soon as they are cooked — many do not take well to being kept warm in the oven for any amount of time.

Choose vegetables that look bright, crisp and firm and never ever overcook them. The test of a truly wonderful cook is her vegetables. When I was first at Upper Grosvenor Street and looking for a cook, Mrs Duckworth was a housemaid there. My children pointed out to me that she was a good cook so I tried her. As soon as I tasted her vegetable soup, I knew that here was the cook for me. I was not wrong.

As a general rule for cooking vegetables the ones which grow under the ground, such as potatoes and parsnips, should be put into cold water, brought to the boil and cooked slowly. The ones which grow above ground should be plunged into boiling water and cooked quickly.

So buy your vegetables and fish and fruit (the same applies to them as for vegetables) on the day of your dinner party. Meat can be bought the day before and many dishes, such as homemade soup and certain sweets and savouries, can be prepared the day before with finishing touches added on the night.

There are some things which you have to buy in bulk or which should always be kept in the store cupboard if you are entertaining on a regular basis. Here's a list of what every hostess's store cupboard should contain.

For your Store Cupboard

salt
ground pepper – black and white peppercorns
grated horseradish
mustards
wine vinegar
olive oil
vegetable oil
tomato purée
dried herbs and spices
garlic
Parmesan cheese
powdered milk
sugar – brown and white
Worcestershire sauce
breadcrumbs
rice
olives
ground and instant coffee
soft drinks
mixers – such as tonic water

And, if you have a freezer, frozen meat, fish and vegetables for emergencies.

Work out your menu carefully in advance, as much as a week before, and check your shopping list carefully too so that you do not forget anything. Once the shopping is out of the way and you've worked out the food aspect of it all, you can think about the table.

The Table

Everyone wants their table to look attractive if they are giving a dinner party, but personally I do not like tables which are too elaborate or over-decorated. At Upper Grosvenor Street I had a beautiful walnut table which could seat 18, or 20 at a pinch. It was beautiful wood so we always used mats for dinner. If you have a lovely table why cover it up with a tablecloth? Of course you must make sure that the mats are matching — mine were organdie — and that the table is well cared for and protected from spills by a good and frequent wax polish.

If you are not lucky enough to have a good polished wood table then there are many pretty tablecloths around. I like elaborate and ornate embroidered or lace tablecloths with matching napkins. If you are worried about the table underneath being damaged by the heat you can buy a heat–resistant felt "blanket", which is not very thick, to go under the tablecloth. The felt is cut to fit your table, reasonably priced and available from large department stores.

If you are having mats on a wooden table then embroidered or plain white damask napkins are attractive. Paper napkins should be a last resort.

The napkins can be folded and placed on the side plate to the left of the place setting. Napkin rings should never be used at dinner parties – they are a sign that the napkins are going to be used again at tomorrow's lunch! They are only acceptable at house parties, where this may indeed be the case.

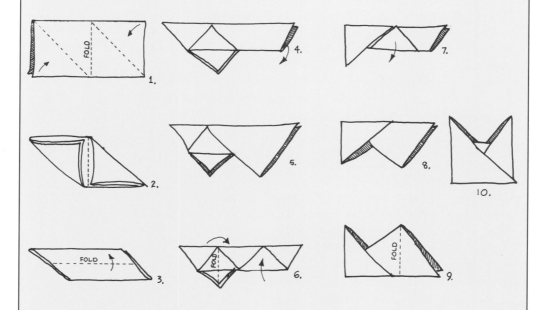

Alternatively you can fiddle your napkin into an interesting shape. Some clever people shape them into "lillies" or "cones"

The easiest shape is the "mitre". Take the napkin and fold it in half, then in half again. Then fold it diagonally and bring the two base points of the triangle together slipping one inside the other. It is easier than it sounds. The mitres may then be put in the middle of each place or on the side plates.

Seating

There are simple rules for where everyone should sit. The host and hostess should sit at opposite ends of the table. The most important male guest to the hostess's right and the second most important man to her left. The most important female guest sits to the right of the host and the second important to his left. In the case of royalty, you put him or her at the head of the table, making them 'host' or 'hostess' for the evening.

Of course it depends on how many people you have to dinner. Ideally with the hostess and host at either ends of the table it should then go man woman man woman around the table. But this is only possible with certain numbers. So if your numbers do not work out ideally, the rule is this: leave the hostess's end of the table as it should be, (the most important male guest still sits to her right and another man to her left) but make the necessary adjustment at the host's end of the table. Whatever happens you should always separate husbands and wives so they are not sitting next to each other. They have not come to your dinner party to talk to each other all night!

For some unknown reason, at official functions, such as a Guildhall dinner, husbands and wives are seated next to each other and I have always wondered why.

Lady Shakerley (Lady Elizabeth Anson) conceived a wonderful new idea called "Party Planners". I ask their help in sending out all my invitations as I then know that they will be in beautiful hand-writing and titles, names and addresses correct. But Party Planners do much more than that, they can arrange entire dinners, providing the food, wine and music, and they have done this for many hostesses.

With any number higher than eight I always put name plates at each seat so that everyone knows their place. With eight or less you can cope with telling everyone where to sit – with more than eight you often do not have the chance before some silly person has already sat down – probably where they should not.

Flowers

I know some hostesses who spend a fortune and hours preparing the table. I am very happy to have flowers but I do not care if I don't. My dining room in Upper Grosvenor Street was very elaborate and having flowers on the table could have been too much.

I often used a crystal and gold bowl as a centrepiece. If you do have flowers on the table only have one arrangement and make sure the bowl is low. I have been to innumerable dinner parties where the table has been smothered in vases with flowers so tall you could not see who was sitting opposite you because of the foliage! This also makes conversation across the table difficult with people ducking and diving in a ridiculous fashion to see who they were actually speaking to. Very irritating.

Always choose flowers that are in season and therefore at their best — daffodils and tiny grapehyacinths in spring and roses in summer. In winter time I really think splashing out on fresh flowers is a waste of money. Use silk ones instead or imaginatively dried flowers and, at Christmas, holly and pine cones.

Lighting

Lights are much more important than flowers. Never have overhead lights. In my house, and here in my flat, I only use wall or table lights. Lights shining down over the dinner table will give women bags under the eyes and four chins. Lights shining up from the table will flatter them. Candles are best, and give a lovely atmosphere. At Upper Grosvenor Street I had two silver candelabras — having three branches each — and I would also have wall lights.

The Cutlery and the Plates

I think the rule here is: use your best. What's the point of having a good dinner service if you do not use it? Many people have beautiful cutlery and dinner services given to them by friends and family as wedding presents but keep them hidden away in cupboards because they are "too good to use". What a waste!

Of course ideally every dinner plate, soup bowl, side plate and dessert dish should match and the cutlery and serving dishes should be of silver. When I entertained at Upper Grosvenor Street I had everything in silver — the cutlery, plates and serving dishes. If you do not have a matching dinner service I really would advise investing in a cheap one if you can. Again go for simplicity. Plain white, perhaps with a very delicate gold or coloured edge, are the most stylish. White plates with white napkins look lovely against polished wood or indeed against a background of a plain coloured cloth.

If you have plain white plates on a pale blue or pink cloth you can afford to have a pretty arrangement of pink or blue flowers at the table's centre and it looks most attractive. If your plates are highly decorated then you should keep the cloth and the centre decoration as simple as possible otherwise it will all look terribly fussy. As for cutlery, again use the best — silver if you are lucky enough to have it. Otherwise you will just have to make the best of what you've got and in all cases it must be sparkling clean and well polished.

For a dinner party for six with four courses — soup, fish, meat, dessert and coffee — you will need six soup bowls and six small plates to go under the soup bowls (you do not want to ruin your table or cloth), six medium sized plates, six large dinner plates, six dessert plates and six side plates for bread, six coffee cups and saucers, a butter dish, sugar bowl and cream jug.

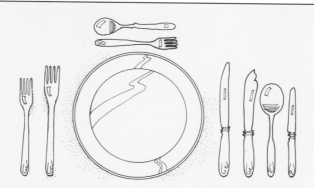

If you are serving at the table you will need (obviously according to what dishes you are giving them) one large soup tureen, one smaller serving plate for the fish, one meat plate, one gravy boat with saucer, three vegetable dishes and one or two little sauce boats with spoons (for example, for redcurrant jelly or onion sauce), salt and pepper condiments and bread basket.

From the cutlery drawer you would need six soup spoons, six fish knives and forks, six dinner knives and forks and six more spoons and forks for dessert, six small knives for buttering bread and six coffee spoons. In addition if you are serving at the table you will need at least three large serving spoons, a souple ladle, a fish slice with spoon and a carving knife and fork or another serving spoon and fork, plus a spoon or slice for the dessert.

Many people are daunted by the prospect of laying the table — where do you put all those knives and forks? Really it is very simple: imagine that you are sitting at the table and place everything according to course, working from the outside in. So if we are to stick to our imaginary dinner of soup, fish, meat and dessert, you would place the small knife for butter, on the right hand side of the plate, inside this would be the soup spoon, inside that the fish knife and inside that the larger meat knife.

On the left of the plate, again working outside in, you would have first the fish fork and then inside that the meat fork. The dessert spoon and fork should be placed above the plates — the spoon pointed to the left above the fork which should point to the right. Do not worry about your left-handed guests — they'll just have to juggle everything around themselves.

It does sound an awful lot of knives and forks and spoons to have on one table and they are very space consuming. I can only say that this is how it is done at formal dinner parties. These are the rules, adapt them as you will. And I must say that a table "properly" laid looks attractive.

The Glasses

This of course depends on what you are going to give them to drink. If you stick strictly to the rules you should give them a different wine to complement each course and a different glass for each. So back to our imaginary meal of soup followed by fish, meat and dessert.

If you serve sherry with the soup, your first glass is a small sherry glass.

Your next glass is a small wine glass with a medium stem to take the white wine which will be served with the fish course.

Glass number three is a larger wine glass with stem for the red wine which will be served with the meat. (Many people – including myself – do not like red wine and prefer to stick with white wine. If this is the case you simply remove their red wine glass and continue filling glass number two.) Finally, a sweet white wine is served with dessert in yet another glass the same size as glass number two.

dessert wine   *red wine*   *white wine*   *sherry*

Just like the cutlery, you place the glasses – working outside in – according to which wine is going to be taken with which course. So with our imaginary meal the sherry glass will be furthest to the right, followed by the white wine glass, then the red wine glass and finally the dessert wine glass.

It may seem a lot of fuss but you really cannot change wines and drink each from the same glass – the taste, bouquet and feeling of the wine is ruined. In fact few people now bother with the sherry or the dessert wine but have two glasses, red and white. It is essential to serve both.

Although it may not seem like it, the different shapes of various glasses are all based on logic. White wine glasses are long and elegant with a long stem – so you can hold it by the stem and the warmth of your hand will not take the chill off the wine.

The bowls of red wine glasses are slightly plumper so you can nestle it in your hand and appreciate the "nose" or aroma of it.

Sherry is served in smaller quantities as it is a fortified wine – hence the smaller glasses. And brandy glasses – which incidentally should never be out on the table before the meal – are balloon shaped so that you can warm it with your hand and appreciate its "nose" or aroma.

Crystal glasses are the most beautiful. At Upper Grosvenor Street we drank from crystal glasses each with a gold rim and monogrammed in gold. If you have crystal glasses – use them! If you do not, many department stores sell very reasonably priced glasses in sets of six. The most important thing is that all the glasses are of the same type - ie, wine, sherry, etc, should match. Non-matching glasses make a table look very messy.

Cocktail glasses these days come in all colours and some extraordinary shapes – for example the ones which have a glass "straw" incorporated in the design. But the basic shape of a cocktail glass remains the same – a tall thinnish stem with a cone-shaped bowl.

Cocktails

Cocktails have the advantage that as well as sounding impressive they often look pretty too if you serve them with fruit or straws. Unfortunately they can work out rather expensive if the ingredients include exotic liqueurs. To economise, buy miniatures of these ingredients rather than a full bottle which will probably sit in the cupboard for months.

My father who spent many years in America loved dry Martinis and always had one or two before dinner. So I include the "recipe" for a Dry Martini here, plus three other favourites, the Pink Gin, Manhattan and Pina Colada.

Dry Martini

Some people say that to make a really good Martini you should simply pour the gin and then wave a bottle of Martini over the glass! I think this is rather a dangerous practice as most of your guests will probably fall over before they reach the dinner table! So I advise the following:

2 measures of gin
1 measure of dry vermouth

Chill the glasses first then put in a little cracked ice. Pour in the gin and vermouth and stir. Only James Bond has his Martinis shaken not stirred. Serve one green olive at the bottom of the glass.

Pink Gin

Very fashionable indeed in my debutante days and increasingly so now. You need:

Angostura bitters
1 measure of gin

Shake a dash of bitters — only four or five drops — into a cocktail glass and roll the glass around so that the bitters coat most of the inside of the glass. Add the gin and some iced water to taste. Leave free from decoration — it looks more stylish in a simple glass.

Manhattan

A very American cocktail. You need:

2 measures of rye whiskey
1 measure of sweet vermouth
Angostura bitters

Put some cracked ice in a glass, mix the vermouth, whiskey and bitters together, then pour over the ice. Stir and decorate with a slice of lemon and a cherry.

Pina Colada

Ideal for people who like their cocktails sweet. You need:

2 measures of cream of coconut milk
2 measures of pineapple juice
1 measure of white rum

Put all the above in a cocktail shaker with some cracked ice and shake until a little frothy. Pour into the cocktail glass, then add a cherry, orange slice and small piece of fresh or tinned pineapple and a pretty straw for decoration.

Fruit cups are not very suitable for dinner parties but I include Pimms here because it really cannot be bettered if you are having a lunch party.

Pimm's No. 1 Club

*Pimms No. 1 cup
chilled lemonade*

Mix the Pimms and the lemonade in a tall cocktail jug. The number of measures depends on the number of people you are entertaining but should always be one-quarter Pimms to three-quarters lemonade. If you want to pep it up a little add a measure of gin too! Add ice, sprigs of mint, slices of cucumber, lemon, orange and apple and serve in tall glasses each with some of the fruit added.

Final reminder – unfortunately cocktails cannot be prepared in advance – you must mix them immediately before serving and they all benefit from being served chilled.

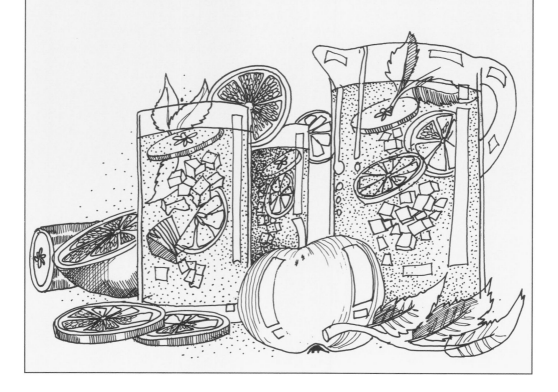

Wine

At first, buying wine for a dinner party can seem a very daunting prospect. The wrong wine with the wrong food can spoil the whole meal. In fact the rules are really very simple and have been devised because some wines go better with some dishes than others.

Very basically, white wine and rosé should be chilled in the 'fridge for at least three hours before serving. Red wines should be served at room temperature and opened an hour or so before the meal to allow the wine to "breathe" – this improves its flavour.

Never put white wine bottles to cool in the freezer – the very low temperature may make them explode! And never put red wines on a hot surface such as a heater to warm – this will ruin the taste.

If you have not had time to chill or warm your wine put the white bottles in a bucket of cold water and the red ones in a bucket of warm – not hot – water. Red wines with very heavy sediment (bits in the bottom of the bottle) need to be decanted into a decanter or jug, but sediment is usually only found in very old and expensive wines. Other red wines do not need to be decanted as long as you have opened them at least an hour before the meal – decanting merely allows the wine to breathe – but personally I think all red wines look much nicer in a decanter.

What goes with what? Basically white wines go with lighter more delicate dishes – red wines are heavier and go with heavier dishes. So you serve white wines with fish, shellfish and white meats such as veal and desserts, and you serve red wine with dark meats such as beef and all game. Poultry is a little tricky. You can serve either a white wine or a light red – whichever you prefer – with chicken or turkey and, for that matter, pork.

To appreciate the different types of red and white wines takes time – but what an enjoyable way to spend your time!

Dry white wines stimulate the palate and so should be served with cold hors d'oeuvres and shellfish.

Dry and medium dry white wines suit all fish, chicken and veal dishes, salads and, if you do not like red, can be taken throughout the meal.

Rosé wines which are medium dry go well with cold hors d'oeuvres, hot fish dishes, veal, lamb and pork.

Light red wines can be served with chicken, game, beef, duck, pork, lamb and cheese.

Medium red wine can be served with chicken, game, beef, duck, pork, lamb and cheese.

Fuller red wines suit game, beef, duck, rich casseroles and cheese.

Sweet white wines complement fruits and sweet desserts.

How do you tell from its label whether a wine is sweet, dry, medium sweet or medium dry? Ask! It is always best, especially when you're first experimenting in entertaining, to ask a good wine merchant to recommend wines to accompany your dinner. He certainly will not be offended — if he's a good wine merchant then he should be happy to show off his expertise. Do not be embarrassed by your lack of knowledge. If you see a bottle of the appropriate colour and appropriate price on the shelf, simply ask, is it dry or medium dry or whatever. If the wine merchant is not very helpful, it may be that he does not know what he's talking about anyway — so go to another shop!

It would be quite impossible to list here the names of all the wonderful wines you can buy but I have listed a few of the most popular and reasonably priced wines to look out for.

Dry white wines — Muscadet, Chablis, Vinho Verde (has a slight sparkle) from Portugal.

Dry and medium dry white wines — Sancerre, Soave, Alsace Riesling, Moselle.

Rosé — Anjou rosé, Californian rosé, Mateus rosé.

Light red wine — Beaujolais, Valpolicella, Californian red.

Medium red wines — wines from Bordeaux (claret), Chianti, Rioja.

Fuller red wines — some Bordeaux wines, Burgundies, Côtes du Rhône, Châteauneuf-du-Pape.

Sweet wines — sweet Hocks, Sauternes.

Coffee and Liqueurs

The coffee you serve at a dinner party should always be fresh and not instant. If you have gone to all the trouble of creating a wonderful dinner you might as well make the extra effort of serving good coffee.

You can make fresh coffee even if you do not have a coffee machine or percolator (you really should have one — fresh coffee is so much nicer than instant even when you're not giving a dinner party!) Warm a large jug, add the appropriate amount of fresh, finely ground coffee and boiling water, cover the jug with a saucer and leave for at least five minutes. Then strain the coffee into small coffee cups.

Brown sugar tastes better with fresh coffee than white and cream much nicer than milk. Some people do not like coffee, but do not feel you have to offer them tea instead. They always offer tea or coffee after dinner in America but I never do. I think tea after dinner is simply awful.

The cost of your dinner party can rise alarmingly if you indulge your dinner guests with a vast array of liqueurs after the meal. Better to stick to crème de menthe, kummel or brandy, a choice of either preferably and, one of the sweeter liqueurs often much preferred by women guests.

I could not possibly list all the world's liqueurs but here are a few of the more popular ones. If you travel abroad, particularly in Europe, you will no doubt come across some that look extraordinary, brightly coloured and sold in peculiarly shaped bottles. Some, I have to say, taste quite revolting to my mind but nevertheless it can be quite fun to bring some miniatures home and try them out in case you make a delicious discovery that you can eventually use on a party night.

Port: Port is fortified wine made from grapes that grow in the northern valley of the Douro river, Portugal, and shipped out from Oporto. Vintage port is a wine that has spent years in its bottle before reaching the table. Wood ports are blends of different wines of varying ages. Some are called ruby — these are a blend of young wines; or tawny — a blend of ruby port and another wine, or simply a ruby port that has matured.

White port is unlike the others. It is a gold colour and made entirely from white grapes. White port is not suitable as an after-dinner drink but chilled it makes a good aperitif, not unlike sherry.

Vintage port is really the only port you should serve after dinner.

Brandy: Brandy is a spirit distilled from wine. It is the most popular of what the French called digestifs – the drinks that aid digestion – so it makes the perfect after-dinner drink. The most famous brandies and the best come from the Cognac region of France, thus called Cognacs.

But there are other French brandies you might like to try – Calvados is an apple brandy that takes its name from the town of Calvados in Normandy, or Armagnac from south of Bordeaux.

Other liqueurs:

Tia Maria – a spicy liqueur, a Jamaican rum based on coffee extracts.

Grand Marnier – an orange-flavoured liqueur.

Drambuie – Scottish liqueur with the flavour of honey and, of course, whisky!

Cointreau – another orange-flavoured liqueur.

Crème de Menthe – bright green and peppermint-flavoured.

Disasters

However good you are as cook or hostess, disasters do happen. Unfortunately they often happen when you most want to impress. Above all try to keep cool, calm and smile, smile, smile!

The worst disasters often happen in the kitchen, out of sight of the unsuspecting guests, so you can repair the damage before they notice. Always keep a few extras in the store cupboard in case you have to stretch the meal. For example if the joint of meat you have bought suddenly shrinks to nothing while cooking – or once you get the piece of meat home it looks far smaller than in the shop – something like stuffed tomatoes will fill them up and make the meal appear more than it is, and also looks attractive. A friend cooking a goose for the first time completely miscalculated the amount of fat in the bird. He was left with an enormous dish of fat and hardly any meat for ten guests, but he quickly prepared a few spicy stuffed apples to make it stretch.

Try to keep some extra vegetables around too – give them three different vegetables instead of two or, if you are giving them hors d'oeuvres, tart up a few cans of soup with vegetables or sherry and give them four courses instead of three.

Another trick – put plenty of Melba toast on the table! If your sauce or soup suddenly turns out to be too salty add some milk or, with soup, a mashed potato and some extra stock so you have the correct thickness.

Overcooked vegetables should be looked upon as a disaster. They taste awful. But you can put some life back into them. Drain them well and put them back into a clean saucepan. Then have them over a very low heat for a few minutes so that as much moisture as possible evaporates. Or you can blend them with butter or a little cream or both plus salt and pepper to make an exotic vegetable purée.

If a sauce suddenly curdles a quick whisk or a few minutes in a blender will usually do the trick.

Meringues can also turn out wrong – they break, crumble or go soggy. If so, break them up into small pieces, mix with cream and fresh fruit such as raspberries, and serve in individual dishes topped with nuts. The guests will not know anything has gone wrong.

Menus

This is not intended as a recipe book but I have included here a few recipes which I have served over the years to my dinner guests. I must emphasise again that I like good, simply cooked food — I really don't think you can beat it and as a guest I'd certainly prefer to be given simple food — which is very good — than dozens of exotic dishes which are bad. I think, particularly, if you are inexperienced in giving parties and have to do everything yourself, the simpler you keep it the better. After each menu I've included the recipes for each dish, all the amounts are given for six people — adjust the measurement accordingly.

Spring Menus

Spring Menus

Quail eggs
Fish salad
Chicken fricassée
Chocolate soufflé

Watercress soup
Salmon trout
Duck with cherries
Pineapple dessert

Vichyssoise
Trout with almonds
Crown of lamb
Bananas & Cointreau

Summer Menus

Summer Menus

Melon

Lobster Thermidor

Fillet steaks with sour cream

Tipsy strawberry ice

Gazpacho

Cold poached salmon

Boeuf Stroganoff

Raspberry water ice

Autumn Menus

Autumn Menus

Borsch
Fish timbales
Roast Pork
Light lemon cream

Hot prawn chowder
Cheese soufflé
Roast pheasant
Chicken livers & toast

Paté
Pasta & Mediterranean sauce
Veal cutlets
Poached peaches

Winter Menus

Winter Menus

Hot consommé
Sole with black grapes
Pot roast partridge
Savoury herring roe

Smoked salmon mousse
Roast turkey
Christmas pudding

Soups and Hors d'Oeuvres

Hot Consommé

Consommé is a clear broth and a wonderfully versatile soup. You can serve it hot in winter or iced and jellied in summer. Add thin strips of vegetables such as carrots or celery — first boiled separately — and it becomes consommé Julienne, or add cooked asparagus tips and it is called consommé Princesse.

Sometimes cooked rice is added or savoury egg custard cut into fancy shapes. Served simply and hot. You can always add a couple of tablespoonsful of sherry for extra flavour.

2 pints brown stock

4 oz lean beef

2 carrots, peeled

1 small onion, skinned and quartered

the white and shell of one egg

1 bouquet garni

salt and pepper to taste

Remove any fat from the stock and trim any fat from the meat. Chop the meat finely and soak in one third of a pint of water for 15 minutes. Put the meat and its liquid, stock, vegetables, crushed eggshell and bouquet garni into a saucepan. Over a gentle heat add the egg white and whisk continuously until a frothy scum starts to form on top. Stop whisking, bring to the boil and remove most of the scum with a large draining spoon. Boil fiercely for one minute then turn heat down and simmer gently for 30 minutes.

Strain the soup through a clean cloth and then reheat — or leave to chill — and add sherry or chosen garnish. Season to taste.

Borsch

(A THICK AND WARMING BEETROOT SOUP)

2 lb cooked but not vinegared beetroot, peeled

1 oz butter

3 large onions, skinned and chopped

$1^1/_2$ pints chicken stock

$1^1/_2$ pints water

$^1/_2$ glass white wine

a little Worcestershire sauce

a little vinegar

1 clove garlic, crushed

salt and black pepper

$^1/_2$ pint single cream

Boil the beetroot for 40 minutes until really soft. Melt the butter in a large pan and fry the onions until soft but not brown. Drain the beetroot and add to the onion with the stock, water, wine, Worcestershire sauce, vinegar, garlic, salt and pepper and bring to the boil. Simmer for 10 minutes. Remove from the heat and mix in a blender for 1-2 minutes. Serve hot or cold adding a swirl of cream just before serving.

Gaspacho

(THE TRADITONAL COLD SPANISH SOUP)

1 medium cucumber

1 lb ripe tomatoes

4 oz green peppers

3 oz skinned onions

2 slices white bread, with crust on, soaked in ¹/₂ pint water

15 oz can tomato juice

3 tablespoons olive oil

3 tablespoons wine vinegar

2 tablespoons tomato purée

1 clove of garlic, skinned and finely chopped

salt and black pepper

Wash and chop the vegetables. Mix all the ingredients in a basin and then, a little at a time, purée in a blender. Place six to eight ice cubes in a bowl and add the soup. Chill until very cold, stir and serve garnished with fried garlic croutons and extra finely chopped green pepper, tomato and raw onion. (Dilute to taste, if necessary, with chilled water).

Watercress Soup

(TASTY AND COLOURFUL)

2 bunches of watercress
1 oz butter
2 medium sized potatoes, peeled and chopped
1 pint chicken stock
salt and pepper
¼ pint milk
3 tablespoons cream

Wash and trim the watercress — reserve a few sprigs to garnish. Melt the butter over a low heat, add the cress and potato and toss gently for 3 minutes. Add the stock and seasoning and simmer for 30 minutes. Sieve or liquidise. Return to the heat, add the milk and bring to the boil, stirring. Cook for five minutes. Just before serving, add a swirl of cream to each bowl and garnish with a sprig of watercress.

Vichyssoise

(CREAMY LEEK SOUP, SERVED CHILLED)

2 oz butter

4 leeks, finely chopped

1 onion, skinned and chopped

2 potatoes, peeled and chopped

2 pints chicken stock

salt and pepper

7 fl oz single cream

chives, chopped

Melt the butter in a large pan and gently fry the leeks and onion in the butter for about 10 minutes until soft but not browned. Add the potatoes and stock. Cook until the vegetables are tender, then sieve or liquidise. Check the seasoning and stir in the cream. Chill. Serve in individual bowls sprinkled with chives.

Melon

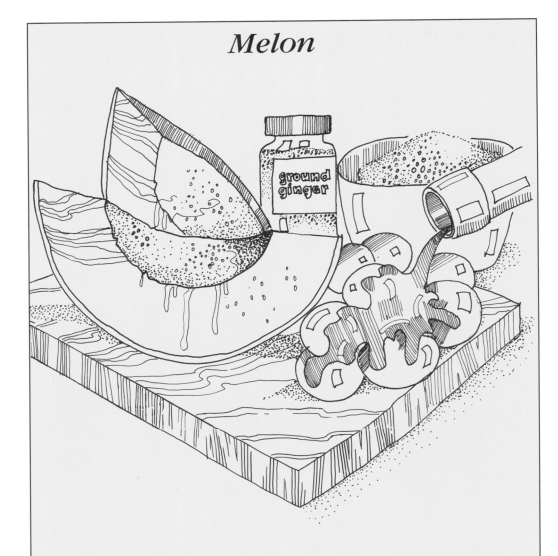

Melon always makes an excellent starter if you either add some port to the cavity of small halves before serving, or serve in wedges with ground ginger and castor sugar.

Melon cocktail can be made by simply mixing cubes of melon — or melon balls made by scooping melon out of its skin with a teaspoon — with other fresh fruits such as raspberries. Sprinkle with caster sugar and a liqueur or sherry and chill. Serve in glasses, or bowls set in crushed ice.

Quail Eggs

These tiny eggs sound and look exotic but are usually reasonably priced and make a delicious, impressive starter. They have a delicate flavour and creamy yolk. Traditionally, they are served hardboiled with brown bread and butter and celery salt. You can also serve them with dips and mayonnaise.

Allow 4 to 6 eggs per person. To boil, put in cold water, bring to the boil and simmer for 3 to 4 minutes. Dunk eggs in cold water, and for ease, peel while warm. However, they look very pretty with their shells on served in "nests" of mustard and cress.

The eggs can also be fried or poached. Serve in small pastry cases or a variety of canapés and vol-au-vents. They are especially good with anchovy, or with grated raw onion and lumpfish roe on toast.

Hot Prawn Chowder

a knob of butter

1 large onion, peeled and chopped

3 medium potatoes, peeled and chopped

salt and black pepper

6 oz peeled prawns, fresh, frozen or canned

1 pint milk

2 oz cheese, grated

Melt the butter and lightly fry the onion for five minutes until soft but not brown. Add 7 fluid oz of boiling water, the potatoes, salt and pepper. Cover and simmer for 20 minutes until potatoes are cooked. Add the prawns and milk and reheat gradually, stirring in the cheese. Garnish with parsley.

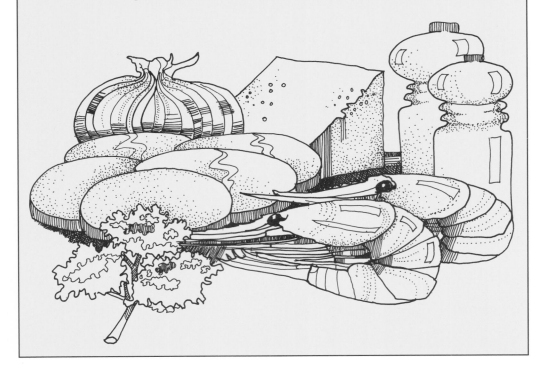

Smoked Salmon Mousse

For this recipe you can use the cheaper smoked salmon pieces or trimmings available from most delicatessens or fishmongers where they sell salmon carved to order.

¹/₂ pint milk
1 carrot, peeled and chopped
1 onion, skinned and chopped
2 oz butter
2 oz plain flour
5 teaspoons gelatine
³/₄ pint chicken stock
4 oz smoked salmon pieces
juice of one small lemon
2 tablespoons mayonnaise
salt and black pepper
¹/₄ pint double cream
parsley and slices of lemon to garnish

Bring the milk to the boil, with the carrot and onion. Remove from the heat and leave to stand for 15 minutes. Melt the butter in a separate saucepan. Stir in the flour and cook for two minutes over a very low heat stirring occasionally, but do not brown. Gradually stir in the strained milk and then bring to the boil, stirring continuously.

Dissolve the gelatine in a little hot stock in a bowl, then add the rest of the stock. Cool. Chop the smoked salmon into small pieces. Fold the stock into the milk sauce, add the salmon, lemon juice, mayonnaise, and seasoning to taste. Beat the cream and fold into the mixture. Pour the mixture into a soufflé dish or individual ramekins. Chill well. Garnish with slices of lemon and sprigs of fresh parsley and serve with milk toast.

Pâté

(EASY, RICH AND DELICIOUS BUT VERY FILLING)

6 oz butter
¹/₂ lb chicken livers, halved
1 large clove garlic, chopped
1 level teaspoon dried thyme
1 level teaspoon dried marjoram
1 level teaspoon dried basil
salt and black pepper
1 tablespoon dry sherry or brandy
paprika pepper
1 bay leaf

Melt 4 oz butter in a frying pan but do not burn. Add the livers and fry gently until they are pinkish brown, about 3 – 5 minutes. Spoon into a blender or processor base and add the garlic, herbs, salt and pepper.

Pour the sherry or brandy into the frying pan, bring to the boil and add to the mixture. Purée for about a minute – less if you prefer a coarser pâté – more if you like the pâté smooth. Empty pâté into a dish and smooth the surface with a knife.

Sprinkle with a little paprika. Place the bay leaf on the surface. In a clean saucepan melt the remaining butter and pour over the top of the pâté. Chill in the fridge for at least four hours before serving with toast, cucumber slices and lemon wedges.

Fish and alternatives

Fish Timbales

(A DELICIOUS TASTE)

1 oz butter
1 oz sieved cornflour
$^{1}/_{2}$ pint fish stock
salt and black pepper
1 lb cooked white fish
2 tablespoons chopped parsley
2 egg whites
parsley sprigs and lemon wedges to garnish

Melt the butter in a pan over a low heat, add the flour, stirring continuously and cook for a few minutes until smooth but not brown. Remove from the heat and gradually beat in the stock. Return to the heat and bring to the boil, stirring all the time. Season and simmer for five minutes. Flake the fish well and add to the sauce with the parsley. Allow to cool slightly. Beat the egg whites stiffly and fold into the fish mixture. Butter individual timbale or dariole moulds and fill almost to the top of each. Cover with buttered greaseproof paper and steam for 20 minutes. Turn out carefully onto individual plates. Garnish with parsley sprigs and lemon wedges and serve with hot toast.

Cold Poached Salmon

1 salmon or salmon trout
3/4 pint water or water and dry white wine, mixed
1 small onion, skinned and sliced
1 small carrot, peeled
1 celery stick
1 bay leaf
peppercorns and salt
2 slices of lemon

Ask the fishmonger to clean the fish, leaving on the head and tail, but removing the eyes. Put all the other ingredients into a pan and simmer for half an hour. Strain and allow to cool.

Place the fish in a deep shallow frying pan and pour over the liquid so that it covers the fish. Cover the pan and cook over a low heat for 10 minutes. The fish is cooked when a skewer easily pierces its thickest side. Serve hot or cold. (Cool in the cooking liquor). Salmon steaks can be cooked in the same way. Serve hot or cold with a hollandaise sauce.

For a really impressive cold dish for a special occasion, salmon and salmon trout can be glazed in aspic. Poach the fish then allow to cool. Remove the skin from the body of the fish, leaving the head and tail intact. Make up 1 pint of aspic jelly according to the directions on the aspic packet. When it begins to thicken, coat the skinned fish with a thin layer. On the layer of aspic lay thin slices of cucumber and radish, sliced olives or strips of pimento, in a decorative pattern. Coat with layer after layer of aspic jelly until the decoration is set.

Fish Salad

2 lb cod fillet (preferably fresh)
a little salt
juice of half a lemon
$1/2$ cucumber
2 tablespoons fresh chopped mint
2 tablespoons fresh chopped parsley
6 tablespoons olive oil
2 tablespoons white wine vinegar
pinch of mustard
1 clove garlic, crushed
pinch of sugar
To garnish:
2 oz peeled prawns
lemon wedges
sprigs of mint and parsley

Clean and skin the fillets and poach in a pan with water, salt and lemon juice until the fish is just cooked – milky white in colour but still firm (about 12 minutes).

Drain the fish and put aside until quite cold. Dice the cucumber. Flake the fish but leave it in coarse pieces. Add the cucumber, mint and parsley. Make the dressing by mixing well the oil, vinegar, mustard, garlic and sugar. Pour dressing over the fish mixture and toss gently taking care the fish doesn't break up. Serve chilled in individual dishes or scallop shells, garnished with prawns, lemon wedges and parsley or mint sprigs. Serve with brown bread and butter.

Cheese Soufflé

6 eggs, separated
2 oz butter
3 tablespoons flour
¹/₂ pint milk
6 oz cheese, finely grated
salt and pepper

Grease an 8-inch soufflé dish. Separate the eggs. Melt the butter in a large saucepan and gradually stir in the flour over a low heat. Cook for two minutes. Slowly add the milk and, stirring all the time, bring to the boil. Cook for 1-2 minutes. Remove from the heat and add the cheese, then the egg yolks, one at a time, and the salt and pepper. Beat well for two minutes. Whisk the egg whites until they are still and form peaks, and fold them into the cheesy mixture. Put the mixture into the soufflé dish and bake at 350°F (180°C, gas mark 4) for approximately 40 minutes until risen and browned.

Lobster Thermidor

(HOT LOBSTER WITH CHEESE AND WINE SERVED IN THE SHELL)

2 lobsters, cooked
2 oz butter
1 small shallot or onion, chopped
2 tablespoons chopped parsley
1 oz flour
¹/₄ pint milk
1 oz cheddar cheese, grated
4 tablespoons dry white wine
pinch of paprika
salt and pepper
mustard
Parmesan cheese
watercress and lemon wedges to garnish

Cut the lobsters in half lengthways with a heavy knife or chopper. Remove and throw away the vein running through the centre of the tail; the stomach, which can be found near the head; and the inedible gills. Remove meat from body. Crack the large claws with a rolling pin and remove the meat with a skewer or very finely pointed knife. (If in doubt, ask your fishmonger).

Chop the pinky-white flesh into bite sized pieces. Melt half the butter in a pan, add the meat and toss over a low heat. In another pan melt the rest of the butter, add the shallot or onion and cook over a gentle heat until soft. Add the parsley and flour, stirring continuously. Gradually whisk in the milk, bring to the boil stirring all the time and cook for 1 minute. Reduce to a simmer and add the grated cheese. Continue stirring and add the wine, paprika, salt and pepper and mustard. Pour the sauce over the lobster in the other pan. Cook over a low heat for four minutes, mixing well. Thoroughly clean the lobster shells and wipe dry. Pour the lobster mixture into the shells, sprinkle with the Parmesan cheese and place under a hot grill until the cheese is bubbling. Serve garnished with the watercress and lemon wedges.

Sole with Black Grapes

4 oz black grapes

4 generous fillets of sole

1 shallot or 2 slices of raw peeled onion

parsley sprigs

salt and pepper

¼ pint dry white wine

¼ pint water

1 oz butter

3 tablespoons flour

¼ pint milk

2 tablespoons cream

Reserve a few grapes for garnish, then peel the rest and remove the pips. Lay the fillets flat in a frying pan. Add the shallot or onion, sprigs of parsley, salt and pepper, wine and water. Cover and poach very gently for 10 minutes. Remove fish carefully, place in a serving dish and keep warm. Reduce the liquid by boiling rapidly for one or two minutes. Remove from heat.

In another pan melt the butter, stir in the flour and cook for two minutes. Gradually stir in the fish liquid and the milk, bring to the boil and continue stirring until the sauce has thickened. Remove from the heat and stir in the cream and the peeled grapes. Pour over the fish fillets and serve garnished with the reserved grapes.

Trout with Almonds

4 trout
seasoned flour
6 oz butter
2 oz blanched almonds
juice of half a lemon
parsley sprigs and lemon wedges to garnish

Ask your fishmonger to clean the fish, leaving the heads on. Wash and wipe them dry. Coat the trout in the seasoned flour. Melt 4 oz of the butter and gently fry two trout at a time for 15 minutes, turning once during cooking. When they are cooked and golden on both sides place on a serving dish. In a clean pan melt the remaining butter, add the almonds and lemon juice and cook until the almonds are lightly browned. Just before serving pour the butter over the fish and garnish with lemon wedges and parsley sprigs.

Pasta and Mediterranean Sauce

salt and pepper

a few drops of oil

8 oz pasta (spaghetti, tagliatelle, vermicelli or shells)

1½ oz butter

2 onions, skinned and chopped

15 oz can of tomatoes

2 oz tomato purée

pinch of marjoram

pinch of sugar

1 clove garlic, peeled and finely chopped

4 oz mushrooms

Parmesan cheese

Bring a large pan of water to the boil, add a pinch of salt and a few drops of oil. Add the pasta and cook for 10 to 15 minutes until almost tender. Drain and toss in ½ oz butter. In another pan fry the onions in 1 oz butter until they are soft but not brown. Add the tomatoes, tomato puree, marjoram, sugar, garlic and salt and pepper. Cover and simmer for 30 minutes. Add the sliced mushrooms and the cooked pasta. Toss well and serve with Parmesan cheese.

Meat and Game

Roast Pork

Make sure the rind of the joint is well scored to help produce a good crackling. Rub the rind with salt and oil and roast for 25 minutes per lb plus 25 minutes for meat on the bone, at 425°F (220°C, gas mark 7). If it is a rolled joint off the bone, reduce heat to 375°F (190°C, gas mark 5) for 35 minutes per lb. Pork should always be cooked very thoroughly. Serve with apple or gooseberry sauce or baked apples stuffed with sage and onion.

Roast Pheasant

For 4 people you will need to cook two – a brace. Ask your butcher to prepare the pheasant. With a knife pierce the skin on each side of the breast and force a little butter in between the skin and flesh. Then cover the breast with strips of bacon fat or rashers of streaky bacon. Sprinkle with salt and pepper. Roast in the oven at 450°F (230°C, gas mark 8) for 10 minutes and then reduce the heat to 400°F (200°C, gas mark 6) and continue cooking for about 40 minutes. 20 minutes before the end of cooking time, remove the bacon fat and baste well. Serve with bread sauce and a thin gravy.

Crown of Lamb

Ask your butcher to prepare a crown of lamb from two pieces of best end of neck, each with about six cutlets. He will need to be given a little notice for this. Make sure the crown is secure with string and skewers. Place in a roasting tin. Fill the centre with foil so the crown keeps its shape during cooking and twist some foil around the exposed bones to prevent burning. Spread the meat with a little dripping, sprinkle with salt and pepper and roast for 30 minutes per lb plus 30 minutes at 350°F (180°C, gas mark 4). After cooking, remove all the foil and hang little cutlet frills on the ends of the bones. The centre of the crown can be stuffed with sausagemeat, sage and onion stuffing or any other good stuffing before cooking. Alternatively, it can be filled with small vegetables just before serving.

Pot Roast Partridge

4 partridges
1 oz butter
4 oz streaky bacon, rinds removed and chopped
4 tablespoons sherry
1/2 pint beef stock
juice of one orange
salt and black pepper
4 oz white grapes, seeded and halved
1 tablespoon cornflour
watercress and orange slices to garnish

Ask your butcher to prepare the partridges for cooking. Melt the butter in a pan and add the partridges. Cook, turning, until brown all over. Lift partridges from the fat and place in a casserole. Add the bacon to the fat and fry until golden brown. Stir in the sherry, stock, orange juice and seasoning. Bring to the boil, pour over the partridges, cover and cook for 1¼ hours at 350°F (180°C, gas mark 4). Add the grapes and cook for another 10 minutes. Place the partridges on a serving dish and put the liquid in a pan over a low heat. Blend the cornflour with a little water and add to the sauce. Bring to the boil, stir until slightly thickened, and pour over the partridges. Garnish with watercress and slices of orange.

Veal Cutlets

2 oz butter

1 tablespoon chopped onion

4 oz chopped ham

1 tablespoon chopped parsley

salt and pepper

4 veal cutlets

$^1/_2$ wine glass Marsala or sherry

Over a low heat, melt $^1/_2$ oz of the butter in a wide frying pan and add the chopped onion, ham, parsley and seasoning. Fry for one minute. Add the rest of the butter and the veal cutlets and fry for about 4 minutes on each side. Add the Marsala or sherry and a little water and simmer for another 5 minutes.

Fillet Steak with Sour Cream

1 oz butter
2 tablespoons oil
1 clove garlic, crushed
4 fillet steaks, weighing about 4 oz each and 1/2" *thick*
2 tablespoons Worcestershire sauce
1 tablespoon grated onion
2 teaspoons chopped parsley
salt and black pepper
1/4 pint sour cream
2 teaspoons grated horseradish
parsley sprigs to garnish

Melt the butter with the oil and garlic in a frying pan. Fry the steaks gently for 2 minutes each side, or 3 minutes if you prefer meat well cooked. Remove the steaks from the pan and keep warm on a serving dish in the oven. Add to the pan the Worcestershire sauce, onion, parsley, salt and pepper. Heat gently, stirring. Add the sour cream and horseradish and heat through without boiling. Pour the sauce over the steaks and serve garnished with parsley.

Chicken Fricassee

2 oz butter
4 chicken breasts, skinned
2 tablespoons plain flour
10 shallots or 3 small onions, peeled and chopped
¹/₄ pint dry white wine
¹/₃ pint chicken stock
parsley sprigs
1 bay leaf
8 oz button mushrooms, halved
1 egg yolk
¹/₄ pint double cream
salt and black pepper

Melt one ounce of butter in a heavy-based casserole over a low heat. Coat the chicken in the flour and sauté in the butter until brown. Remove the chicken pieces and keep warm.

Meanwhile, add the onions to the butter and fry until soft but not brown. Stir in the wine and stock, parsley and bay leaf. Return chicken to the casserole, bring to the boil and then simmer, covered, over a low heat until the chicken is cooked. In a clean pan melt the rest of the butter and over a low heat, fry the mushrooms until just cooked. Mix together the egg yolk and cream and stir into the chicken casserole. Then add the mushrooms. Heat gently but do not boil. Season to taste and serve with boiled rice and a watercress salad.

Duck with Cherries

1 bacon rasher, rind removed
1 small onion
1 small carrot
1 small celery stick
1 1/2 oz butter
1 tablespoon plain flour
1 pint chicken stock
2 bouquets garni
2 tablespoons tomato purée
salt and black pepper
1 roasting duck
1 orange
2 oz caster sugar
1 wine glass sherry or port
1 lb stoned red cherries

Chop the bacon, onion, carrot and celery. Fry the bacon in 1 oz of the butter on a low heat. Add the chopped vegetables and fry until browned. Stir in the flour and continue frying and stirring until brown. Remove from the heat and gradually add 1/2 pint stock, stirring continuously. Return the pan to a medium heat and stir until the sauce thickens. Add the bouquets garni, tomato puree, salt and pepper. Simmer for 1 1/4 hours, stirring occasionally, then strain, skim off any fat and put to one side.

Meanwhile, rub the breast of the duck with butter, prick the skin with a fork and sprinkle with salt. Put the duck in a roasting tin, surrounded by 1/2 pint stock. Roast for 30 minutes per lb at 375°F (190°C, gas mark 5).

Thinly pare the rind from the orange and cut into thin strips. Put the strips with the juice of the orange, the sugar and the sherry or port in a pan. Over a low heat allow the sugar to dissolve, then add the cherries. Cover and simmer for 5 minutes. Strain and put the cherries to one side, but keep hot. Add the orange juice to the gravy mixture and reheat stirring well.

Place the cooked duck on a serving dish surrounded with the cherries. Pour over some of the sauce and serve some separately in a sauce boat. Serve with new potatoes and minted peas.

Boeuf Stroganoff

1 1/2 lb rump steak, thinly sliced
salt and black pepper
3 level tablespoons flour
2 oz butter
1 onion, skinned and very thinly sliced
1/2 lb button mushrooms, sliced
1/2 pint single cream

Remove any fat from the steaks, then beat with a rolling pin to flatten out. Cut into thin strips about 2 inches long. Dip the pieces of steak in seasoned flour and fry in 1 oz of butter for 5 minutes, turning the meat frequently. Do not overcook the meat. Meanwhile, fry the onions and mushrooms gently in another pan with the rest of the butter for a couple of minutes until the onions are soft but not brown. Add to the meat. Pour in the cream and stir well over a low heat, until warmed through, but do not boil. Serve with boiled rice and a green salad.

Roast Turkey

Choose a plump bird. An 11-14 lb bird will feed 13 to 15 people, a 15-20 lb bird 16 to 30 people. Frozen turkeys should be allowed to thaw out slowly in the fridge over 2-4 days. Stuff the neck and body of the bird. Chestnut stuffing is traditionally used for the neck and sausage meat for the body. Fold the wings under the body and tie the legs together. Cover the breast with streaky bacon rashers or bacon fat and spread the remainder of the exposed skin of the bird with some soft dripping or butter. Sprinkle the bird with salt and pepper.

Wrap the bird in foil and cook at 450°F (230°C, gas mark 8) for $2\frac{1}{4} - 2\frac{3}{4}$ hours for a bird weighing up to 10 lb, 3 hours for a bird weighing up to 14 lb, $3\frac{1}{2}$ hours for a bird weighing up to 18 lb and $3\frac{3}{4}$ hours for a bird weighing up to 22 lb. Half an hour before the end of the cooking time, unwrap the foil leaving the top of the bird free for browning and baste well. Serve with cranberry sauce, bread sauce, sausages and bacon rolls.

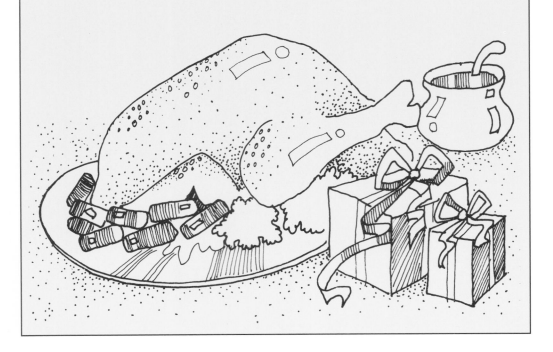

Desserts and Savouries
Christmas Pudding

2 oz self raising flour

4 oz fresh white breadcrumbs

4 oz shredded suet

1/2 lb soft brown sugar

1/4 lb sultanas

1/4 lb raisins

3/4 lb currants

grated rind one lemon

1 tablespoon fresh orange juice

1 oz mixed peel

1/2 small apple, peeled and chopped

1/2 teaspoon mixed spice

1 pinch each nutmeg, cinnamon, ginger

1 oz chopped skinned almonds

2 large eggs

1/4 pint stout

2 tablespoons brandy

Mix the dry ingredients thoroughly. Then add the dried fruits, rind, juice, peel, apple, spices and nuts. Beat the eggs, add the stout and brandy, mix again and pour over the dry ingredients. Mix very thoroughly. The mixture should have a fairly soft dropping consistency and fall off the spoon when tapped. If it is too dry, add a little milk — or extra stout.

Cover the bowl with a cloth and leave overnight. Grease a 3-pint pudding basin, pour in the mixture to the top, cover with greaseproof paper and then wrap tightly in a pudding cloth. Steam for five hours. Keep in a cool, dry place until required and steam for another 1½ hours or more before serving with cream and brandy butter.

Bananas and Cointreau

(VERY RICH BUT DELICIOUS)

4 bananas

1 oz butter

lemon juice

1 oz sugar

1 teaspoon cinnamon

2 tablespoons Cointreau

2 tablespoons fresh orange juice

1 carton double cream

Peel and split the bananas in half lengthways. Place flat side upwards in a buttered serving dish and sprinkle immediately with lemon juice to prevent browning. Mix the sugar and cinnamon and sprinkle over the bananas. Pour on the Cointreau and orange juice and marinate for two hours. Dot with butter and bake in the oven at 350°F (180°C, gas mark 4) for 15 minutes.

Serve hot with double cream.

Pineapple Dessert

1 large pineapple

8 oz vanilla ice cream

^{1}/4 pint double cream, whipped

2 oz butter

3 tablespoons brandy

2 oz brown sugar

Split the pineapple in half lengthways. Using a sharp knife, scoop out the pineapple flesh, chop roughly and divide into two bowls. Mix the ice cream and cream carefully with half the pineapple flesh, and spoon back into one of the pineapple shells. Freeze for 2 hours. Melt the butter in a pan, add the brandy and half the sugar. Cook stirring for one minute. Add the other half of the pineapple flesh and cook for two minutes, stirring continuously. Pile the mixture into the other pineapple shell. Place in a small roasting tin. Sprinkle with the remaining sugar and bake in the oven at 350°F (180°C, gas mark 4) for 20 minutes. Serve hot and cold pineapple halves side by side.

Raspberry Water Ice

(REFRESHING AND EASY TO MAKE)

4 oz caster sugar

1 lb raspberries

2 pints water

lemon juice

Sprinkle the sugar over the raspberries and leave for two hours. Then mash them and squeeze through muslin or a very fine sieve. Add the water and a dash of lemon juice. Mix and freeze, whisking two or three times whilst freezing.

Tipsy Strawberry Ice
(CREAMY AND DELICIOUS)

8 oz fresh strawberries
¹/₄ pint double cream, softly whipped
dash of vanilla essence
1 tablespoon Maraschino liqueur
2 oz sugar
strawberries for decoration

Purée and sieve the strawberries, then mix well with all the other ingredients. Pour into a freezing container and put in the freezer part of the fridge for 1 hour. Then remove and beat the mixture again until smooth. Freeze until firm. Decorate with fresh strawberries.

Poached Peaches

1 lemon
8 oz sugar
¹/₂ pint dry white wine
8 medium sized peaches

Remove the lemon rind, without any white pith and cut into very thin strips. Squeeze out the juice. Put the sugar and wine into a saucepan and stir over a low heat until the sugar has dissolved. Add the lemon rind and boil for 3 minutes. Put the peaches in boiling water for one minute to make peeling easier. Peel them, then plunge them into cold water with the lemon juice to prevent them from browning. Drain the peaches, add them to the syrup and cook gently for 20 minutes, turning over occasionally. Leave them to cool in the syrup, then cover and chill.

Chocolate Soufflé

(RICH BUT ALWAYS A FAVOURITE)

3 eggs, separated
¹/₄ pint milk
3 oz caster sugar
¹/₂ oz gelatine
3 tablespoons water
2 oz dark chocolate, melted
¹/₂ pint double cream
chocolate chips

Take a 6-inch soufflé dish and wrap a band of greaseproof paper around the outside so that it protrudes 2 to 3 in above the top of the dish. Mix the egg yolks, milk and sugar in a bowl over boiling water and whisk until pale, thick and frothy. Dissolve the gelatine in the water and lightly whisk into the egg mixture with the melted chocolate. Cool. Whip the egg whites and cream in separate bowls. Fold the cream into the egg mixture, and then the egg whites. Pour into the soufflé dish so that the mixture comes well above the top of the dish and leave to set in the fridge or a cool place. Just before serving carefully remove the paper and sprinkle with chocolate chips.

Light Lemon Cream

(A ZINGY TASTE)

3 eggs, separated

4 oz caster sugar

grated rind and juice of 2 large lemons

2 level teaspoons gelatine

4 tablespoons double cream

lemon slices

Whisk the egg yolks with the sugar until thick and creamy and add the lemon juice. Dissolve the gelatine in a little water and whisk into the lemon mixture. Beat the egg whites well until they form peaks. As the lemon mixture begins to set, fold in the egg whites and the lemon rind with a metal spoon. Pour into individual serving dishes. Leave to set and decorate with double cream and lemon slices.

Chicken Livers and Toast

4 rashers streaky bacon, rinds removed

black pepper

4 oz chicken livers

1 oz butter

4 slices bread

a little chopped parsley

Cut the bacon rashers into two lengths and sprinkle with pepper. Roll the pieces of bacon around pieces of chicken livers, secure each with a cocktail stick and fry quickly in butter on both sides. Melt the rest of the butter and fry the bread, cut into fingers, until golden. Serve the liver rolls on the bread fingers, garnished with parsley.

Savoury Herring Roe

12 herring roes
1 oz butter
2 slices of bread
salt and pepper
lemon juice
parsley sprigs

Wash and dry the roes. Melt ½ oz butter in a pan and, over a low heat, fry the roes for about 10 minutes until golden. Drain on kitchen paper. Cut the bread into fingers, melt the rest of the butter and fry the fingers until golden. Put the roes on the bread fingers, season, sprinkle with lemon juice and garnish with parsley sprigs.

Diary

Diary

Location: ....

Date: ....

Occasion: ....

Guests present _____   Menu_____

Unable to attend   Wine

Table decoration_____

_____Seating plan_____

Comments_____

Diary

Location: ....

Date: ....

Occasion: ....

Guests present _____   **Menu** _____

Unable to attend   **Wine**

Table decoration _____

Seating plan

Comments

Diary

Location: ....

Date: ....

Occasion: ....

Guests present _____ **Menu** _____

Unable to attend **Wine**

Table decoration _____

Seating plan

*Comments*_____

Diary

Location: ....

Date: ....

Occasion: ....

Guests present _____   Menu_____

Unable to attend   Wine

Table decoration _____

Seating plan

Comments

Diary

Location: ....

Date: ....

Occasion: ....

Guests present _____

Menu_____

Unable to attend

Wine

Table decoration_____

_____ _Seating plan_ _____

Comments _____

Diary

Location: ....

Date: ....

Occasion: ....

Guests present _____   **Menu** _____

Unable to attend   **Wine**

Table decoration _____

Seating plan

Comments

Diary

Location: ....

Date: ....

Occasion: ....

Guests present _____

Menu _____

Unable to attend

Wine

Table decoration _____

_____ *Seating plan* _____

....

....

....

....

....

....

....

....

....

Comments _____

Diary

Location: ....

Date: ....

Occasion: ....

Guests present _____

Menu _____

Unable to attend

Wine

Table decoration _____

Seating plan

Comments

Diary

Location: ....

Date: ....

Occasion: ....

Guests present _____ **Menu** _____

Unable to attend **Wine**

Table decoration _____

Seating plan

Comments

Diary

Location: ....

Date: ....

Occasion: ....

Guests present _____   **Menu** _____

Unable to attend   **Wine**

Table decoration _____

Seating plan

Comments

Diary

Location: ....

Date: ....

Occasion: ....

Guests present _____ **Menu** _____

Unable to attend **Wine**

Table decoration _____

_____*Seating plan*_____

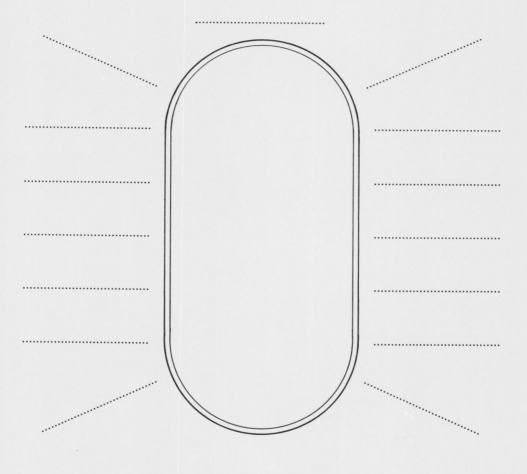

*Comments*_____

Diary

Location: ....

Date: ....

Occasion: ....

Guests present _____ **Menu** _____

Unable to attend **Wine**

Table decoration _____

_____*Seating plan*_____

....

....

....

....

....

....

....

....

....

*Comments*_____

Diary

Location: ....

Date: ....

Occasion: ....

Guests present _____ | ## Menu _____

Unable to attend | ### Wine

Table decoration _____

Seating plan

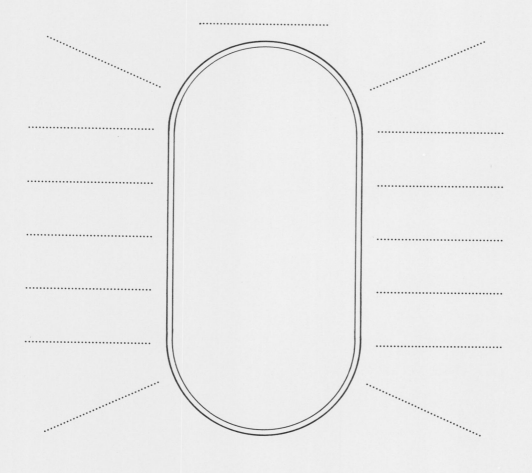

Comments

Diary

Location: ....

Date: ....

Occasion: ....

Guests present _____ **Menu** _____

Unable to attend **Wine**

Table decoration _____

_____ *Seating plan* _____

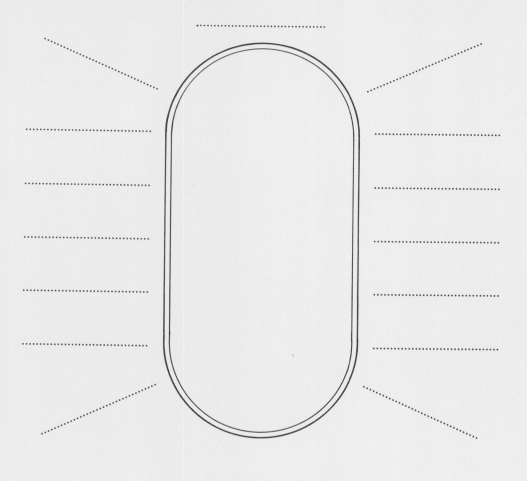

Comments _____

Conversion Tables

Conversion of Temperatures

°FAHRENHEIT	°CENTIGRADE
250°F	121°C
275°F	135°C
300°F	149°C
325°F	163°C
350°F	177°C
375°F	191°C
400°F	204°C
425°F	218C
450°F	232°C
475°F	246°C

To convert Centigrade temperatures to Fahrenheit, multiply by 9, divide by 5 and then add 32. Conversely, to turn Fahrenheit temperatures into Centigrade, subtract 32, multiply by 5 and divide by 9.

Conversion of Metric Weights

OUNCES	GRAMS
1 oz	*30 g*
2 oz	*60 g*
3 oz	*85 g*
4 oz; ¼ lb	*115 g*
5 oz	*140 g*
6 oz	*180 g*
8 oz; ½ lb	*225 g*
9 oz	*250 g*
10 oz	*285 g*
12 oz	*340 g*
14 oz	*400 g*
16 oz; 1 lb	*450 g*

Conversion of Liquid Measures

AMERICAN	IMPERIAL
2 tablespoons	*1 oz*
¼ cup or 4 tbsp	*2 oz*
⅓ Cup	*2⅔ oz*
½ Cup	*4 oz*
⅔ Cup	*5⅓ oz*
¾ Cup	*6 oz*
1 Cup	*8 oz*
1 Cup	*8 oz*
1¼ Cup	*10 oz*
1½ Cup	*12 oz*
1⅔ Cup	*13⅓ oz*
1¾ Cup	*14 oz*
2 Cup; 1 pint	*16 oz*

Index to Recipes

Soup and Hors D'oeuvre

Borsch   92
Gaspacho   93
Hot consommé   91
Hot prawn chowder   98
Melon   96
Pâté   100
Quail eggs   97
Smoked salmon mousse   99
Vichyssoise   95
Watercress soup   94

Meat and Game

Boeuf stroganoff   117
Chicken fricassee   115
Crown of lamb   111
Duck with cherries   116
Fillet steaks with sour cream   114
Pot roast partridge   112
Roast pheasant   110
Roast pork   109
Roast turkey   118
Veal cutlets   113

Fish and alternatives

Cheese soufflé   104
Cold poached salmon   102
Fish salad   103
Fish timbales   101
Lobster thermidor   105
Pasta and mediterranean sauce   108
Sole with black grapes   106
Trout with almonds   107

Desserts and Savouries

Bananas and cointreau   120
Chicken livers and toast   127
Chocolate soufflé   125
Christmas pudding   119
Light lemon cream   126
Pineapple dessert   121
Poached peaches   124
Raspberry water ice   122
Savoury herring roe   128
Tipsy strawberry ice   123